P9-EMR-768

Praise for *Outthink the Competition*

"Instant information, immediate price comparison, and an expanding breadth of customer choice are thrusting business leaders into a new era of competition. Kaihan's fresh message opens minds and motivates strategic change in an era that demands change. If you want to 'outthink the competition,' read this book."

—Robert Bloom
U.S. CEO, Publicist Worldwide, retired;
Author of *The New Experts* and *The Inside Advantage*

"We have been using Kaihan's concepts for years now to grow our company and they just work. *Outthink the Competition* packs his principles into an easy-to-apply framework that will have your competition guessing at every turn. Read this before your competitors do."

—Roy Hessel
CEO and founder, EyeBuyDirect

"Having a great product and team is no longer enough. Leaders need to be able to understand, anticipate, and creatively manage the competition and world markets. Kaihan helps create a template to *Outthink the Competition* and this playbook is in a form that business leaders can apply today."

—Michael Minogue
Chairman, President, and CEO, Abiomed Inc.

"*Outthink the Competition* packages a vast swath of fundamental strategic principles into a practical framework for the modern-day business leader. It shows that insights of Sun Tzu and other historical strategic minds of lineage are even more relevant competing today."

—Mark McNeilly
Author of *Sun Tzu* and *The Art of Business*

"The rules of business have changed dramatically. How you win tomorrow will be radically different from the past and few have their pulse on the emerging era of business competition as firmly as strategist Kaihan. Read this book or be left behind."

—Josh Linkner
New York Times bestselling author of *Disciplined Dreaming*;
CEO, Detroit Venture Partners;
Chairman and founder, ePrize

"Kaihan continues to demonstrate the power and persuasiveness of storytelling. His compelling insights from contemporary successful strategic outthinkers are grounded in the centuries-old wisdom of the narratives of political leaders, generals, scientists and even sports heroes—all innovators in their field. The often counterintuitive lessons will resonate and stimulate any leader navigating the new 24/7 global challenges of today . . . and more importantly, tomorrow."

—Paul Kennedy

McKinsey & Company Partner, retired

OUTTHINK THE COMPETITION

OUTTHINK THE COMPETITION

HOW A NEW GENERATION OF STRATEGISTS SEES OPTIONS OTHERS IGNORE

KAIHAN KRIPPENDORFF

WILEY

John Wiley & Sons, Inc.

Published by John Wiley & Sons, Inc., Hoboken, New Jersey.
Published simultaneously in Canada.

For general information on our other products and services or for technical support, please contact our Customer Care Department within the United States at (800) 762-2974, outside the United States at (317) 572-3993 or fax (317) 572-4002.

Wiley publishes in a variety of print and electronic formats and by print-on-demand. Some material included with standard print versions of this book may not be included in e-books or in print-on-demand. If this book refers to media such as a CD or DVD that is not included in the version you purchased, you may download this material at http://booksupport.wiley.com. For more information about Wiley products, visit www.wiley.com.

Library of Congress Cataloging-in-Publication Data:

Krippendorff, Kaihan.
Outthink the competition: how a new generation of strategists sees options others ignore/ Kaihan Krippendorff. –1
p. cm.
ISBN: 978-1-118-10508-5 (hardback)
ISBN: 978-1-118-16384-9 (ebk)
ISBN: 978-1-118-16385-6 (ebk)
ISBN: 978-1-118-16386-3 (ebk)
1. Strategic planning. 2. Competition. 3. Creative thinking. 4. New products. I. Title.
HD30.28.K753 2012
658.4'012—dc23 2011029034

Printed in the United States of America

10 9 8 7 6 5 4 3 2 1

CONTENTS

ACKNOWLEDGMENTS

When writing my first book in 2004, I thanked my wife, Pilar Ramos, for giving up weekends in the sun so that I could write. Seven years later, our family grown, her sacrifices are four times as large. I thank her and our three beautiful children—Lucas, Kaira, and Makar—for understanding how important this book was to me and allowing me the space to finish it. I am glad I will be back home more often now, for fútbol games, movie nights, and giggles. I also thank my father, Klaus Krippendorff; my mother, Sultana Alam; and my stepmother, Marge Thorell—for being unconditionally interested and encouraging.

My agent, Laurie Harper, warned me that I would get to write only one book. After the first one, a work of love you write all alone, you become a team with deadlines and process. She was right, and I could not continue to do what I love without the outstanding professionals around me who support my work, including Laurie, who has guided and represented me for nearly 10 years now; Megan Fuhrmeister, who has become a daily partner, helping me think through my messages and produce the weekly articles that formed the building blocks of this book; and Maggie Stuckey, whose ability to understand, untangle, and weave order from such a breadth of subjects, while staying true to my voice, made this book possible.

My colleagues and collaborators also made essential and innumerable contributions, providing the practical experience to help ensure that this book and the Outthinker Process presented here actually work in real life. I thank Nadia Laurinci, Lolita Albuquerque, Satoko Gibbs, Helmut Albrecht, Robin Albin, Susan Drumm, Thaddeus Ward,

Lynette Gilbert, Jenny Sarang, Patrick Thean, and my friends at BlessingWhite, AltaGerencia, and *Harvard Business Review Latin America*.

In preparing this book, I have drawn on experiences with many clients who have, whether they are aware of it or not, enriched this book by allowing me to work with them. Some of these include Mike Minogue, Shannon Wallis, Shannon Banks, Tony Crabb, Salomon Sredni, Marc Speichert, Enrique Riquelme, Juan Pablo Michelsen, Michel Correa, and Juan Jose Gonzales.

I also enjoy the guidance, support, and mentorship of several forward thinkers and am especially grateful to Paul Kennedy, Sabrina Herrera, Jack Barker, Verne Harnish, Joseph Miller, Josh Linkner, and John Copeland.

Finally, about 50 busy entrepreneurs and CEOs agreed to spend time with me to discuss their organizations, strategies, and thought processes. Their names are sprinkled throughout this book, so I will not list them again here. But to them all I say, thank-you for allowing me and all those who read this book an opportunity to learn from you.

PART 1

The Foundation

> *A new scientific truth does not triumph by convincing its opponents and making them see the light, but rather because its opponents eventually die, and a new generation grows up that is familiar with it.*
>
> —Max Planck[1]

Every domain—war, science, business—evolves through periods of radical change, through revolutions. Such times divide us into thinkers and outthinkers. Outthinkers step outside of the accepted paradigms in which thinkers operate. They act differently because they see the world differently. Revolutions unfold in a predictable four-step pattern that ultimately leads to outthinkers toppling thinkers.

1. First, people grow rigid, adopting a set way of doing things. They fall into a pattern—1, 2, 3—and stop looking for a better way.
2. Then, someone (an outthinker) questions what others have accepted and finds a new strategy (a "fourth option").
3. The new strategy proves superior.
4. The competition tries to copy but can only do so slowly.

We are in the midst of such a revolution right now in the domain of business. The winners of today are competing with a new set of rules and are flustering their traditional competitors as a result.

CHAPTER 1

Evolution through Revolution

One thing is clear: If our ideas and thoughts matched perfectly with what goes on in this world; and if the systems or processes we designed performed perfectly and matched with whatever we wanted them to do, what would be the basis for evolving or creating new ideas, new systems, new processes, new etc.? The answer: There wouldn't be any!

—Colonel John Boyd[1]

I cannot tell the story I want to tell, about a man who almost lost his job but emerged a hero. The head of a little-known business unit lost in a global conglomerate, and lackluster growth, he decided to try something new. Like all innovators, he endured the ridicule of his peers, who could simply not see the logic underlying his unorthodox new strategy. The dissent grew so strong he was almost forced out. But just in time things started to change. Revenue picked up, profit margins expanded, and the company began taking notice. Within two years, his seemingly radical strategy had more than doubled the size of his business.

This man is a client as well as a friend, and so confidentiality prevents me from sharing the details of his story. Instead, let me tell you another. This one you will certainly recognize and it makes precisely the same point.

In August 2004, a two-year-old company with a brash idea was preparing to go public. Everyone in Silicon Valley and most investors around the world were debating the same questions: What is Google worth? Should I invest?

In hindsight, of course, we know the answer. Shares that were $85 at the IPO trade are at about $500 today. But in the summer of 2004, even smart, forward-looking investors could not predict Google's success.

"I'm not buying," Stephen Wozniak, cofounder of Apple, told the *New York Times* in the weeks before Google's IPO. "I'm not buying. Past experience leaves the taste that a few people—never ourselves—will make out the first day, but that it's not likely to appreciate a lot in the near future or maybe even the long future."[2]

Jerry Kaplan, a well-known Silicon Valley entrepreneur who proved himself as the principal technologist at Lotus and went on to launch multiple companies, said, "I wouldn't be buying Google stock, and I don't know anyone who would. . . My experience is that when you step outside the bounds of normalcy, you are in very dangerous territory. A lot of things can go wrong."[3]

Why the hesitation? Because the company's explosive growth—from $439.5 million in 2002 to $1.46 billion in just one year—looked to many investors too much like the rise-and-fall trajectory of Netscape, which had started out far ahead of slower incumbents but was soon defeated by Microsoft's Internet Explorer. Was Google heading the same way?

Just months before the IPO, the narrative of Google's slowing revenue growth was setting in: in the quarter that ended June 2004, that growth was just 7.5 percent, compared with 27 percent the prior quarter. Randy Komisar, a well-known technology entrepreneur, said, "You can't hide the fact that this thing is slowing down. There was a year of hypergrowth, and then it rolled over."[4]

A look at the company using traditional financial analysis supported the view that the Google IPO would fizzle. But look at what Google has achieved since going public. It has positioned itself at the center of the Internet world. It has transformed the advertising industry. It is the only large, profitable, publicly traded company to average more than 100 percent annual growth over the past 10 years. Its $27 billion IPO valuation in 2004, once viewed by educated investors as excessive, just a few years later is overshadowed by its market value of more than $140 billion (2010). And along the way it created thousands of millionaires.

Why didn't Google fizzle, as a lot of smart people predicted? Because its leaders looked hard at the competition and the standard model of doing things and saw there was a new way—a better way—of doing things.

It seems revolutionary now, partly because Google created a business not even imagined just a couple of decades ago. But Google was, in fact, following in some well-established footsteps, dating back centuries. At its core, finding this better way is nothing more—and nothing less—than a bold new way of thinking.

In all domains of competition—from business to sports to war—breakthrough success evolves through the same pattern. First the players fall into a routine, adopting the same practices. They are the thinkers who think inside the accepted paradigm. Then outliers, a few innovators who defy the standard practices, emerge. We will call them outthinkers, because that's what they do. Outthinkers don't outmuscle their competitors, or outspend them; they out*think* them.

The thinkers first dismiss the outthinkers, then they ridicule them; eventually they realize the outthinkers have figured out something new and then they try to copy them. But if the outthinkers play their game right, by then it is too late. The outthinkers have won.

Outthinkers in War

In the military domain we see breakthroughs come about when an outthinker appears on the scene. Rather than perfect prevailing tactics, the outthinker takes a fresh perspective on the battlefield. This perspective reveals as obvious strategies and methods that to others seem unorthodox, even crazy.

Hannibal's Defeat

Around 200 BC, when Scipio Africanus was asked by the council of Rome to lead Rome's defense against Hannibal, he already knew that the traditional approach would be ineffective. A series of military leaders had tried and failed to put an end to Hannibal's attacks. So Scipio Africanus set aside the obvious strategies. Instead, he turned his back to Hannibal—literally—and led his men into what is now Spain, laying siege on New Carthage (modern-day Cartagena).[5]

Why would he make such a seemingly backward move? Because Scipio understood better than his predecessors the strategic value of doing so. Carthage, the north African power, supplied Hannibal's campaign through New Carthage. So when Scipio overcame New Carthage, he cut Hannibal off from his supply lines. It was this counterintuitive choice—to turn his back on his target and instead attack New Carthage—that led to Hannibal's fall and, arguably, to the end of Carthage itself.

Genghis Khan's Victory

The European knights awoke before dawn. They climbed up into heavy, well-crafted armor and mounted oversized horses. They gathered their foot soldiers and archers and walked toward the battlefield.

As they lined up facing the trees through which their adversary would soon emerge, they felt great confidence. They were fighting close to home, so supplies were within a few miles; in contrast, their opponents had stretched their supply lines across hundreds of miles. The European knights had studied the arts of warfare from books and through years of formal training; their aggressors were savages, with tactics that had evolved little from those of early hunters. The knights didn't see how they could lose.

But when the Mongols blasted out of the woods, the knights' confidence turned to surprise and then fear. They had never before seen an enemy fight like the one they were facing now.

The Mongols made three key strategic choices that flummoxed traditional armies.

1. *Surround rather than confront.* At a time when battles were fought by two armies lined up face to face, the Mongols preferred instead to surround their opponents. What led them to this formation was not calculated strategy but instinct. The Mongols viewed warfare as hunting, so they fought the same way they hunted—by surrounding their prey, herding them toward the center, and then showering them with arrows.
2. *Shoot from horses rather than from the ground.* It was a then-accepted military theory that archers must shoot with their feet firmly planted on the ground to ensure accuracy. But the Mongol soldiers had spent years training to hunt with bows from horseback and could shoot accurately even while galloping.
3. *Use a full cavalry rather than foot soldiers.* Armies at the time were composed of a mixture of archers, foot soldiers, and cavalry. Battles were typically fought by deploying each in sequence: first archers would launch volleys to weaken their opponents, then foot soldiers would march in to engage in close combat, and finally cavalry rode their horses into battle, usually by flanking, to finish the job. But in the Mongol army, every soldier rode a horse, and the knights of Europe had no idea how to engage such an army.

The central lesson of the Mongols' success—and the lesson that this book intends to make clear—is that to win any strategic game, be it war, business, or chess, you must make a few strategic choices that will so disorient your competition that they will not be able to respond effectively.

What makes a difference and provides an advantage is doing what your competitors will not do or will not respond intelligently to. In that sense, the Mongol strategies provide a perfect model for today's business leaders. Rather than match the traditional strategies of their adversaries, they diverged from tradition and, in so doing, forced their enemies into a dilemma: Do we stick with what we know, or do we change our approach? Do we break the straight fighting lines our men have practiced for years to surround our opponents? Do we start shooting from horseback even though we have never practiced this before? Do we tell our foot soldiers to go home and leave the fighting to the cavalry? The armor-clad knights could not adapt with sufficient speed—even if they had wanted to—and they found themselves sticking to their standard methods, with disastrous results.

Outthinkers in Sports

We see the same pattern at play in sports. An outthinker takes a new perspective on the game which reveals a new approach. This new approach proves superior but the competition, bound by training and tradition, are slow to adapt.

Dick Turns His Back on Tradition

In 1968 Dick Fosbury literally turned his back on tradition. The 21-year-old U.S. Olympian ran toward the high bar just as all of his competitors had. But as he approached his mark, he twisted his back awkwardly and flopped over it backward.

At the time of the 1968 Olympics, every gold medal winner in recent history had cleared the high bar using one of three forward techniques: the straddle, the Western roll, or the scissors jump. Every coach of every winner had trained their athletes in the same type of strategy: jumping over forward. Every expert and every textbook agreed.

As it turned out, it was the young college student, not the seasoned experts, who was proved right. Fosbury cleared 7 feet 4¼ inches, winning the gold medal and beating the world record by a full 2.5 inches. When the Olympics ended, perhaps even before, athletes around the world rewrote their training programs. They had to learn to master Fosbury's strange technique. By 1980, 13 of the 16 Olympic finalists were using the *Fosbury Flop*.[6]

Passing Over Tradition

We can only image what Dwight Eisenhower and Omar Bradley were thinking as they watched the Notre Dame–Army at West Point football game from the Army bench on November 1, 1913. Years before either fought in a war or became four-star generals, or before Eisenhower became a U.S. president, they had played for West Point's football team. Neither player mounted the field that day because their opponent, Notre Dame University, a poor Catholic college from Indiana that was virtually unknown in the East, was devastating the mighty Army team.

The game shocked Army—and indeed the entire sports world. The next day the *New York Times* report of the game began, "The Notre Dame eleven swept the Army off its feet on the plains this afternoon, and buried the soldiers under a 35 to 13 score."[7]

Notre Dame won not by playing the game better but by playing an entirely different game, with an innovation that fatally flustered Army—the forward pass. The *New York Times* explained:

> *The Westerners flashed the most sensational football that has been seen in the East this year, baffling the cadets with a style of play and a perfectly developed forward pass, which carried the victors down the field thirty yards at a clip.*[8]

To today's fans, the idea of passing a ball forward to a teammate may not appear noteworthy. But in 1913 it held disruptive power because it forced opponents into a dilemma. Using the game they were used to, Army was getting killed. Should they change, and if so, how?

The Army team had mastered a form of football that resembled rugby, with players making close contact. Winning depended on strength and weight, gaining inches at a time. But when Notre Dame's quarterback tossed the ball over the pile of players in the second quarter, launching it 30 yards into a teammate's open arms, Army's skill at muscling the ball forward by inches was suddenly irrelevant.

To respond to Notre Dame's innovation, Army had to spread its players out on the field. All that did was make it easy for Notre Dame to run with the ball through the gaps. The media reported that the ball was in the air half of the time and that Army's players stood confused, unsure whether to move out for a pass or step in to stop a run.

What Made the Notre Dame–Army Game a Turning Point in the Evolution of American Football? Three Factors Came Together That Day

1. *New rules:* In 1913 the rules were changed, and teams were allowed to pass farther than the existing 20-yard limit. Suddenly the forward pass was more than an alternative to running the ball; it was an entirely new strategy. All of Notre Dame's touchdowns in the 1913 game came from forward passes, most of them longer than 20 yards.
2. *Tactical asymmetry:* Notre Dame had mastered the forward pass, whereas Army was entirely unfamiliar with it. This created an uneven match not unlike Genghis Khan's use of mounted archers against traditional mounted swordsmen.
3. *Media:* The national media houses were based in the East and primarily covered East Coast games. So Notre Dame and others in the Midwest had been able to develop the forward pass in obscurity.

Notre Dame's tactical innovation ushered in a new era of American football. Over the next 20 years, players increasingly practiced the forward pass, the shape of the ball changed to something longer and narrower, and the rules were adapted to reflect the new strategic situations the forward pass made possible. The system slowly adjusted to a new strategy.

The Lesson for Outthinkers in Business

> First they ignore you, then they laugh at you, then they fight you, then you win.
>
> —*Mohandas Gandhi*[9]

The Fosbury Flop and the Forward Pass; Mongol Dominance and Rome's Successful Rout of Hannibal—They All Reflect the Very Same Pattern

1. People grow rigid: they accept that a certain way of doing things (I call this the *1-2-3*) is the best and stop seeking better options.
2. Someone questions what others have accepted and finds a new strategy (I call this the *fourth option*).
3. The new strategy proves superior.
4. The competition tries to copy it but can only do so slowly.

There are four challenges, then, for outthinking your competition:

1. You must first recognize where rigidity has taken hold.
2. You must then find a new strategic option (a fourth option) that others ignore.
3. You must figure out whether this new strategy is superior.
4. You must slow your competitors' ability to copy your innovation.

From this outthinker perspective, let's look at Google again. Dissect how Google built its powerful foundation, and we see the exact same pattern that led Genghis Khan and Notre Dame to victory.

Step	Google Case
1. People grow rigid: they accept a set way of doing things to be the best and stop seeking better options.	Investors, bankers, and Internet experts come to believe that the Internet search business is outdated. It has become an undifferentiated commodity business. They believe the Internet winners will be portals, megasites that provide a breadth of Internet content to users with one access point. Internet behemoths like Yahoo! and AltaVista are similarly convinced. They abandon their traditional search business to become portals.
2. Someone questions what others have accepted and finds a new alternative.	Larry Page and Sergey Brin, two Stanford University students, remain infatuated with Internet search. They develop a new way to structure the search process that filters the most popular websites toward the top of a list of search results. It measures a website's popularity by the number of other sites that link to it. They name the search engine Google and market it to Internet portals, convincing them to outsource their search activities to this simple, pure search service.

(*continued*)

(continued)

Step	Google Case
3. The new way proves superior.	Google results are superior to its alternatives. Soon portals around the world sign deals with Google to outsource their search business. Google's offering is designed to be an obvious choice for portals. Portals can simply direct the search queries its users enter in the search pane to Google, which produces results and feeds these back to the portal. Google appears exclusively interested in doing search (a business portals are happy to exit) showing no intentions to sell advertising, which would put it in competition with its own customers. When Yahoo! and AltaVista sign deals to outsource their search to Google, Google instantly becomes the largest search engine in the world.
4. The competition tries to copy it . . . but can't.	In 2003 Google launches AdSense and starts selling advertising directly to customers. As soon as Yahoo! learns of this, it cancels its contract with Google and returns to its previous search partner to offer a compelling alternative to Google. Other portals do the same. But by this time, Google has already taken a lead too long to close in on them quickly. Customers have grown accustomed to Google's search results and now seek it out, leaving whatever portal they have first landed on. Furthermore, because the Google engine learns with each search, it has now gathered experience none can match. This virtuous cycle—more visitors create better searches, attracting more visitors—compounds its advantage over copycats. Today, Google generates more than 95 percent of its revenue from selling advertising on its search business.

Conclusion

Great armies, athletes, and companies win by seeing new strategic options that adversaries are unable to respond intelligently to. To win, then, you want to:

1. See where the competition has grown rigid.
2. Identify new alternatives.
3. Test and refine the new alternatives to reach one or more that are superior.
4. Slow competitive efforts to react.

You need not think like an outthinker to survive. You can work harder and move faster within the old paradigm, but this is like rowing more forcefully while your neighbor has put up a sail. The thinkers will continue rowing and will make progress, but in the end, the outthinkers will sail past effortlessly, going with the flow and adjusting to the new paradigm.

The winds have shifted. A new generation of outthinkers has emerged. This book will show you how to play like an outthinker—how to put down your oar and put up your sail.

CHAPTER 2

Today's Business Revolution

A man newly risen to power cannot acquire greater reputation than by discovering new rules and methods.

—Machiavelli, *The Prince*[1]

Google was not the first to defy current thinking and surprise knowledgeable critics. Most breakthrough companies do this. At the time of their founding, few experts thought that Walmart, Microsoft, IBM, Southwest Airlines, or Dell would succeed, let alone have such a transformative impact on their industries. This is because each of these companies appeared at a revolutionary time and were led by outthinkers, people who thought outside of the prevailing paradigm and embraced new strategic options that others had dismissed. These were people who saw that the old rules were expiring and embraced a new path.

This is what we would today call a paradigm shift, a phrase now so familiar that many have lost sight of its origins.

It was physicist Thomas Kuhn who introduced the notion of paradigms and paradigm shifts in his groundbreaking 1962 paper, *The Structure of Scientific Revolutions*. The word itself, meaning a model or pattern, is not new; it dates back to the sixteenth century. But it was Kuhn, in his study of the history and philosophy of science, who used the term *paradigm* to encapsulate all the established theories of one particular science at one particular time. He called the existing paradigm *normal science* and theorized that scientific progress happens when something new and significant is spotted that doesn't fit into the normal pattern. At that point, a revolution—a paradigm shift—is occurring. Although Kuhn used it only in reference to hard science, the phrase *paradigm shift* has entered the popular vocabulary to mean any major shift in technology, thinking, or practice. One thing we have learned is that successful leaders are able to shift paradigms with agility. This helps them outthink the competition.

Such a paradigm shift is under way today. Its signals may be weak, but if you listen carefully, you will hear it calling out to you. A new cadre of leaders is listening. Apple, Facebook, Amazon, and even some incumbents like AT&T, Microsoft, and L'Oreal, are adjusting their strategic approach to a new world. Beyond the spotlight, hundreds of other innovative outthinkers are waking up to the new world. These innovators include WebMD, Vistaprint, Rosetta Stone, Blue Nile, Tesla Motors, FedBid, Rave Mobile, Valley Forge Fabrics, inVentiv Health, Husk Power Systems, ePrize, and Genomma Lab; you will meet them all in the following pages.

Studying the paths of breakthrough companies, we see they are ruled by the same pattern we saw in Chapter 1, in the stories of breakthroughs in war and sports. That pattern, you may recall, looks like this: The competitors go rigid (they fall into the predictable pattern of 1-2-3), relying on a set way of doing things; then one company launches a strategy that cuts against accepted dogma, creating the fourth option. The fourth option proves successful, yet competitors are unable to respond intelligently. This gives the innovator a competitive buffer in which to grow and, possibly, dominate.

The Foundation of Great Companies

Pick any company that has produced an extended run of breakthrough results,* and you will find its breakthrough rests on the foundation of a

---

* I specifically looked for large companies (with more than $2 billion market capitalizations) that have the highest 10-year average annual revenue growth, are profitable (EBITDA profit margin in excess of 10 percent), and produce a 5-year average return on equity in excess of 10 percent.

completely new idea that contradicts the prevailing beliefs and habits of their peers. They were, in a word, outthinkers.

Company/Outthinker	**. . . pursued**	**. . . while its peers were**
Google	focusing on search	evolving into internal portals
Netflix	delivering movies to homes via mail	renting movies from their stores
Sohu.com	building a search business for the Chinese market	focusing first on developed markets
Research in Motion	using the abandoned pager network for the first BlackBerry	building 2G and 3G devices
Intuitive Surgical	marketing surgical devices (a robotic arm) to patients	exclusively marketing to surgeons
eBay	enabling customer-to-customer commerce	enabling company-to-customer commerce
Apple	focusing on aesthetics and design	pursuing technical performance
Southwest Airlines	providing low-budget travel using a point-to-point model	offering high-end service using a hub-and-spoke system
Dell	selling directly to consumers	selling through retailers
The Home Depot	enabling people to "do it yourself"	selling to professional contractors

In each case and in hundreds more, we see that greatness begins when a company sees a strategic option that others ignore and decides to embrace it. Their competitors have grown comfortable with the status quo and stick to obvious, proven approaches. Breakthrough companies seize such moments of competitive rigidity.

In the chapters that follow, we will look at these innovative companies in detail and analyze what they are doing and why it's working. Here in this chapter, I want to use a broad-stroke approach to describe some powerful trends, not bound by industry or by company size, that are thrusting us into a new competitive era.

Nine Trends Transforming Our World

When Henry Ford began producing the Model T, most people viewed it as simply a new, inexpensive car—but his innovation would transform so much more. By proving the superiority of mass production, which coincidentally was able to cut the price of an automobile by 60 percent, he inspired a major shift in business. Soon, industry after industry changed from collections of small workshops into a few huge factories.

It's not overstating the matter to say that Ford opened up an entirely new era. Because of him, organizational structures changed radically. Corporations were now made up of divisions managed by a central headquarters that used complex reporting structures and monitored key performance indicators.

Starting with Ford, the basis of competition shifted from craft to economies of scale, from talent to asset intensification. That has remained largely unchanged to this day. The existing paradigm, what Kuhn would call the normal science phase, gives established companies certain tangible, sustainable sources of advantage. In addition to superior economy of scale, they have exclusive access to critical sources of supply. We have lived with this formula for decades, with managers and strategy experts tweaking our understanding of this paradigm but not altering it in any significant way.

But several forces are pushing us beyond the Ford paradigm.

1. The Erosion of Economies of Scale

Previously, a company that wanted to create a new product would have to invest millions to build or retool the factory. Today that company can go to Alibaba.com and find a manufacturer ready to provide the product with minimal incremental cost. In other words, with a few mouse clicks and e-mails, an entrepreneur today can achieve the economies of scale that used to require months of planning and millions of dollars.

That same entrepreneur can build the rest of her business at little or no cost. She can get free business cards from Vistaprint and free hosting service for her website, which she can design on her own. She can also get a phone number and e-mail fax service for a few dollars per month.

The way to wealth was once to build a factory so big that no one could match your investment; to standardize parts and platforms so that no one could touch your volume; to establish a brand so widely recognized that no one could afford to pull customers away. For more than a century, industrial conglomerates have depended on such economies of scale to keep their competition at bay. Today that advantage is eroding. Even in production-heavy industries, of which there are fewer, factories grow smaller, more specialized, and they are easily turned on and off. Products grow more customized, turning standardization into liability. Niche brands pop up and, at very little cost, pick off small segments of the market from incumbents who invested decades in building mass loyalty. A new form of competition that draws strength from sources other than scale is emerging.

2. Acceleration

As economies of scale slip away, they are making room for a historic acceleration in the pace of business competition. Cycle times are shortening and the pace of competition is accelerating.

Not only can entrepreneurs start companies at a radically lower cost, they can do so at a fraction of the time once required. It took Walmart 27 years to reach $30 billion in revenue. It took Amazon.com 16 years to do the same, and Google did so in just 13. Skype was founded less than eight years ago (in 2003), yet today it's the world's largest carrier of transnational telephone calls. Companies that went public in the 2000s reached $30 million faster, 18 months faster on average, than those that had had their IPO in the 1990s.

Today conventional wisdom about the time needed for a product launch is being shattered. One of my clients—a global spirits company—used to launch one new product every few years. It was accepted in that industry that launching new brands was a risky, expensive bet that required careful deliberation. But when we analyzed the economics of new product launches, looking at the actual payoff potential of new products versus the costs of developing and launching—costs that were dropping rapidly—we saw they should be launching many more. Today they launch in one year the number of new products that they used to launch in a decade.

This trend is hitting industry after industry. I have clients in pharmaceuticals, consumer products, technology, and financial services that are ramping up product launches, embracing what they call rapid prototyping. They are, in effect, doing in their industries what Google has been doing in online services: launching a continual stream of products before they are fully tested (that is, as betas), seeing how the market responds, and adapting to the market's reaction.

3. Disaggregation

In 1999, I was intrigued by a research paper that proposed that companies and entire industries would soon disaggregate into smaller parts. The paper was ahead of its time, but its vision is now, a decade later, becoming real.

Another innovative thinker, Harvard Business School professor Shoshana Zuboff, wrote that the era of economies of scale is giving way to what she calls *distributed capitalism*. In her view, the "myriad ways in which production and consumption increasingly depend on distributed assets, distributed information, and distributed social and management systems"[2] is transforming the nature of business competition. Where factories, distribution channels, and marketing were once concentrated in a few places by a few companies, all of these are now fragmenting into distributed constellations.

Today, customers can customize cars (such as Toyota's Scion), sneakers (from Nike), their own romance novels (from www.YourNovel.com), and radio stations (through Pandora) to get precisely what they want from the manufacturer, not what the supplier decides to push onto the shelves. Parts are pulled as needed from disparate suppliers and warehouses for assembly. This is driving, and is driven by, a fragmentation and reorganization of entire industries, from media to pharmaceuticals.

Companies that are winning today are achieving levels of productivity and profitability that are impossible using traditional organizational models. I compared about 20 outthinkers to their less successful peers (more detail in Part 2 and Appendix A) and found that the outthinkers generate nearly twice the profit per employee.

What produced such a dramatic difference? Not simply their ability to charge more or extract greater productivity from their employees. Those two factors can explain only a little more than 25 percent of the difference. I believe the other 75 percent comes from organizational fragmentation, companies breaking apart what they used to do in-house and instead doing them through partnerships and commercial relationships.

For example, Bharti Airtel, India's leading wireless provider, was struggling to hire telecom engineers to build their network fast enough to keep up with the exploding demand for wireless services in their country. The company decided to adopt a radical approach: it outsourced the construction and management of its wireless network to Ericsson and Siemens. As a result, Bharti is now able to produce profit margins higher than most Western telecom companies even though their average revenue per customer is just 10 to 15 percent of that of comparable firms in the developed world.

4. *Free Flow of Information*

Information, once controlled by the powerful as a way to maintain their power, is now slipping between their fingers. Global data flows are growing by nearly 50 percent per year.[3] More than 150 million new people connected to the Internet in China in 2009. Facebook has more than 500 million members, a population that would make it the third-largest country in the world.

Consider that in 1995, less than 3 percent of the world's population had a cell phone and less than 1 percent was online. Today, more than 50 percent of the world's population has a cell phone and more than 25 percent are online. More people (4.6 billion) have access to cell phones than have access to toilets (4.3 billion).[4] Today, people are able to access and share information with a freedom unimagined a decade ago.

This puts more power in customers' hands and wrestles control away from the hands of marketers.

5. The Death of the Middleman

The free flow of information is leading to the death of the middleman.

Take a look at Netflix. I fell in love one night when I stopped a movie I was watching to wash dishes in the kitchen before I tiptoed upstairs to make sure the kids were asleep and then continued the movie seamlessly from the spinning bike in my bedroom. The future has arrived! Almost any movie or show I want, where and when I want it.

Alas, I fear, Netflix will soon break my heart. And it's an American icon that is warning me: American Airlines (AA).

You see, middlemen are dying. Sabre, the former AA subsidiary that is now an independent global distribution system (GDS) supplying travel agencies and online travel agencies with ticket and pricing information, recently announced it was raising the rates it charges on AA tickets. This move was an escalation of a battle that has been brewing between airlines and GDSs. Just before the holidays in 2010, AA pulled its fares from online travel agency Orbitz. Just before New Year's, another online travel agency, Expedia, pulled AA flights because of a dispute. What is provoking the animosity, and what does this have to do with Netflix?

Underlying this competitive dynamic is the lowering cost of coordination. Airlines once valued the service GDSs provided: consolidating fares in a searchable manner to consumers. It cost less for airlines to allow independent coordinators to do this job than to do it themselves.

Now the calculus has reversed. Technology and online consumer habits have changed to the point that airlines can efficiently sell directly to consumers, and consumers can search across airlines for free. (Bing's flight search engine, which pulls fare information often directly from airlines' systems, is a great example of this.) Airlines would rather you search on a free service and then click through to their websites to book your seat. This allows them to up-sell you extra luggage, more legroom, and other once-free services that they increasingly depend on for profits.

So the for-profit middleman, the consolidator and coordinator, is under pressure because every day it grows easier and cheaper for providers to do the job themselves. In a disaggregated world, players and information come together fluidly, as needed, at little cost. The middleman's job is being replaced by a more efficient model. I bet the private equity firms who bought Sabre wished they had foreseen this dynamic.

A major force that is pushing Netflix's buttons is the competition from cable and Internet providers. Today's consumers have many viewing options. For example, the Windows Cloud, Verizon's FiOS, and Comcast's Xfinity all provide more access to on-demand movies, which can be watched from any room in the house. These companies usually provide Internet services as well, which is how Netflix offers its customers instant streaming. However, if people can get the same movies on any of their TVs and computers, and only have one bill, then how long will it be before they ditch the mail-away movie?

Back on my spinning bike, watching my movie, I realize Netflix once served a purpose. It helped Time Warner, Disney, and other content owners reach consumers they could not have reached before. But Netflix is going to face mounting pressure. The copying cost that once kept studios from wanting to do it on their own is falling, while the payoff of competing with Netflix is rising. Starz, a movie content owner, currently has a deal to distribute through Netflix, but it will soon expire. The renewed deal, if there is one, will certainly involve a much higher price.

In a 2010 *New York Times* article on Netflix, Time Warner chief executive officer (CEO) Jeff Bewkes slammed Netflix, calling it a small-time organization with a business model that can't work. Bewkes is quoted as saying, "It's a little bit like, is the Albanian army going to take over the world? I don't think so."[5]

Netflix may continue to have an edge for a while longer, but a new era of competition is emerging and Netflix will only survive over the long-term if it adapts and becomes something different, more valuable, than simply a middleman. This is not to say the company will not have its time in the spotlight—just as AOL, TiVO, and Vonage did before being marginalized by traditional cable operators. Coordination costs are falling, and middlemen need to watch out.

6. *Self-Organized Citizens and Customers*

In early 2011 we heard a great deal about the notion that the revolutions in Tunisia and Egypt were made possible by Twitter and Facebook. It's a compelling idea. How, after 30 years of firm-handed rule, could Egyptian President Mubarak have faced the prospect of losing power?

Surely other factors are in play—shifts in global power, macroeconomic pressure, and demographic changes—but it does feel as if social media has finally passed a point of critical mass, ushering in a new era. A new type of organization has emerged.

But Egypt and Tunisia may just be the beginning of a new order of things. The free flow of information, disaggregation of organizations, and the death of middlemen are all playing into a shift in power away from those who control into the hands of the masses who can now coordinate themselves. The masses evolve into complex adaptive systems, like the stock market or ant colonies, and collectively command ever more power.

In a recent survey, CEOs cited the "development of technologies that empower consumers and communities"[6] as one of their top concerns for the next five years.

Later in this book, we will look at the specific mechanics by which social media unlocked these two revolutions and how consumer revolutions are now a real possibility.

7. *The Shift in Power Toward the Developing World*

Three years ago, when my wife took on responsibility for international (i.e., non-U.S. and non-European) public and regulatory affairs for a global financial institution, her role was viewed as peripheral. The action, everybody knew, was in the developed world. After all, those nations produced most of the company's revenue and attracted most of its management attention. Just three years later, the entire view has shifted. Her team now outnumbers her U.S. and European counterparts, and her company's top management personnel are flying into India and China frequently. She was, by luck or intuition, ahead of the curve.

Over the next decade, the developing world will contribute more to global growth than the developed world. That has not happened since the discovery of the New World 200 years ago. Some predict that by 2050, developed countries will have a lower share of global gross domestic product (GDP) than they had in 1700.

Procter & Gamble has famously announced plans to add 1 billion new consumers to its ranks. One of my clients, an equally ambitious consumer products giant, has similar goals. To achieve this, the company must win a significant chunk of the rapidly growing consumer base in the developing world.

This trend is not only for large companies to think about. At a workshop I conducted for a company that operates an online coupon site, we generated more than 100 potential growth strategies. After we weeded them down through several rounds of discussion, India landed at the top. This company must enter India to realize its aspirations. If they wait, they fear an Indian competitor will emerge. Companies large and small are arriving at the same conclusion: a new focus on the developing world is essential.

But as these companies look over the wall and consider how to enter, they are finding equally eager eyes looking back. Companies in the developing world are aggressively pursuing plans to expand into (and often buy their way into) the developed world.

During a trip to Mumbai, I kept my eyes open for the famed Tata Nano—the cheapest car in the world. To be honest, I don't think I saw one, but then again, I'm not sure I would recognize it crammed between moto-rickshaws and the tiny black taxicabs that looked like holdovers from the Soviet era, all of which were madly swerving around pedestrians.

But I know they are out there, because everyone is talking about them. Indian businesspeople I spoke to brought it up regularly in conversation as a symbol of India's emerging flavor of innovation. Everyone is picking apart this marvel, hoping to answer one question: Why did this happen in India?

I was conducting a workshop with Hermann Simon, known as an advocate for what he calls *hidden champions*—companies (mostly German) that you have never heard of but that dominate a global niche like making glass for museum cases. He was proud to say that about half of Tata's components are manufactured by German companies.

And that fact just agitates our need to answer the question: If much of the technology for the Tata Nano is manufactured in Germany, why was this innovation born in India?

What we are witnessing with the Tata Nano is what is commonly referred to as *reverse innovation*, a process that begins by focusing on the need for low-cost products for countries like India and China and then adapting that innovation for the developed world.

If a German car company was given the challenge of developing the cheapest car in the world, the result would most likely be a car priced just under the competition and with just enough stuff to still give it the feel of a high-quality German car. But by understanding what price tag they had to beat to capture the Indian market, Tata was able to engineer a vehicle that caught everyone by surprise—the customer, with a price tag that was half of the closest alternative ($2,000 per car), and the engineering community, with a product that featured smaller wheels, a unique mix of materials, and a movable steering wheel to reduce the cost of having to adapt it to different driving customs.

India offered the perfect environment to introduce the Tata Nano—it has a need and the Tata Nano can fill it. What a perfect example of how a well-organized business can look at its current technology or service and see how it can use reverse innovation to create something new and needed.

Developing-world companies, although still operating under the radar, are winding up. Here's an example: while Caterpillar from the United States and Komatsu from Japan are the recognized leaders in construction equipment, 9 of the industry's 12 largest manufacturers of wheel-loaders (the second-biggest selling piece of construction equipment) are Chinese. And their success is not due only to sales within China, a large and growing market; they also supply a third of the wheel-loaders in emerging markets outside of China. Such high-volume, low-price competitors are ramping up, learning, generating customers, and building brands.

Over the next 10 years we can expect the economic center of gravity to shift from the developed world toward the developing one.

8. A Rising Global War for Talent

If the menu was not in Mandarin, I could have sworn I was sitting in a cool restaurant in New York's West Village. Servers strutted like models between candlelit tables. Over the bar hung a giant chalkboard listing an eclectic wine menu. Toward the entrance stood a chef, dressed in white, in front of a display of 40 or 50 rare cheeses from France and Italy.

A Chinese businessman and I, introduced by a mutual friend, were talking about management training. His company specialized in leadership education, and he was describing how his firm and his Chinese clients are changing their view on training local managers. I was in my usual mind-set, hunting down innovative growth strategies, but soon realized he was coming at it from an entirely different perspective. His greatest challenge was not finding new customers or introducing new offerings; it was recruitment. How could he best focus his firm's growth so that he did not run into the trap, already facing so many Chinese companies, of not being able to recruit enough people?

Another client of mine, who runs a private equity fund in China, called me for our weekly 10 PM coaching session. But instead of talking about the usual challenges—where the revenues will come from, how we can grow faster—she was concerned about how to find the human resources to meet the growth. She needs CEOs who know the local market for her portfolio companies. She needs bankers to help manage the deals.

In Latin America I hear the same thing. Even in the United States, in the midst of a recession, I find my friends and clients are having trouble recruiting the level of talent they need, particularly people who know R&D and strategy and who can lead organizations. In a recent McKinsey Global Survey, business leaders cite a global talent war as one of their key challenges.

This is emerging as a top issue because when you compete for talent today, you are increasingly competing globally. There are equally hungry and exciting companies vying for the person whose résumé you are looking at right now. They are pulling from across the country and across the world. The war for talent is increasingly becoming a global, rather than a regional, fight.

9. Global Network Volatility

We are competing in a more volatile world. Who would have thought that mortgage troubles in Nevada would lead to the collapse of Iceland's financial system or that a small protest in Tunisia would swell into regionwide revolutions that toppled entrenched governments and spiked global oil prices?

Goods, capital, information, and people are flowing more freely, creating an interconnected network in which small changes in one place can produce radical shifts on the other side of the world. Over the past 10 years, trade flows between countries have grown 50 percent faster than global GDP. Cross-border capital flows have grown 300 percent faster. Only 1 in 10 U.S. dollars today is a physical note, one you can touch and fold into your wallet. Cross-national social groups are forming that rival the size of entire countries.

This global interconnectedness, and the volatility that accompanies it, is not a temporary trend. Some 63 percent of executives surveyed by McKinsey in 2010 believe it will become a permanent feature of the world economy.[7] Companies that can make volatility work to their advantage will win. Those who hold on to old strategies will be hobbling themselves. There are no more lone islands to run to. Everything is connected.

Conclusion

Combine these nine shifts and we begin to see a fundamentally new basis of competition emerging. Kevin Constello, president of Ariba, an innovative technology firm that offers collaborative business commerce solutions, calls it a *new model for business*. The companies we see winning today are adjusting to this new reality quickly. They've stopped clinging to economies of scale; they move faster, they scatter, they use the free flow of information to create advantage, they are disrupting the middleman, they let customers self-organize, they think and hire globally, and they embrace, or at least understand, the heightened volatility in which we compete.

PART 2

The New Outthinker Playbook

All things are changing: and thou thyself art in continuous mutation and in a manner in continuous destruction, and the whole universe too.

—Marcus Aurelius[1]

I love to listen to innovators talk, from the chief executive officer (CEO) of a multibillion-dollar corporation to the start-up entrepreneur to the world-changer bringing electricity to rural India. I especially love listening to the stories they tell. It is through stories, after all, that innovators sell their ideas. And I have discovered that their stories also let us look at what is behind their success.

Over the past 10 years, I've had the honor of meeting a number of creative business leaders who have amazing stories. When I sat down and thought about everything I had learned from them, a picture of modern corporate strategy began to emerge, a picture in which the traditional background was fading away in favor of an intensely colored foreground of new ideas. Could I define exactly what was happening, and could I find a way to make that available to other business leaders? I decided to conduct a research program that would, with scientific rigor, analyze and codify what these innovators were doing. (Details of the research and analysis are presented in Appendix A.)

As it turned out, the research verified my hunch: the most successful innovators are using strategies that more traditional companies would never have imagined. They are creating an entirely new playbook.

The Old Playbook Is Out of Date

I use the metaphor of playbook to summarize a company's strategic behavior because it is instantly recognizable, even to those who don't follow sports. Every sports team has its playbook—a collection of a few tested strategies that always seem to work. The playbook says, "Whenever we face situation X in a game, we will do Y, because we know it works. If we do these things consistently, and execute them well, we'll win."

Even if they are not literally written down somewhere, those key strategies are so deeply ingrained that the players and managers automatically put them into play immediately upon the situation arising. Because strategy Y has been successful in the past, they will do exactly the same thing when situation X comes up in the next game—and the next, and the next, and so on. Then when one day the strategy *doesn't* work, they repeat the same thing, only more aggressively, with desperation.

The exact same thing happens in business. In their search for market share and profitable growth, companies tend to settle on using just a few strategies. Because they work, these strategies are repeated year after year, becoming the company's playbook.

Over the Past Several Decades, Companies Have Primarily Built Competitive Advantage with Four Familiar Strategies

1. Achieve customer captivity.
2. Secure preferential access to resources.
3. Build economies of scale.
4. Adopt best practices.

In 2004, at the start of my research program, my colleagues and I began to see a shift away from these traditional sources of advantage. Today it's clear that this shift is not only real but that it's accelerating. Among successful innovators, two of the traditional strategies (economies of scale and best practices) are fading into the background and being replaced with completely new ones. For anyone who hopes to grow a company, the implications are profound.

A New Playbook Is Emerging

One very significant finding came out of my research. When we categorized the narratives that today's winners and losers used to describe their competitive efforts, we found that the winners tended to repeat the same five narratives. Translated into strategies, these five are:

1. Move early to the next battleground.
2. Coordinate the uncoordinated.
3. Force two-front battles.
4. Be good.
5. Create something out of nothing.

In the chapters that follow, we will look at these strategies in detail and watch as some very innovative companies use them to great effect.

- **Rosetta Stone:** In 2005 this company was practically unknown. Seven years later it has emerged as the world's leading provider of language learning solutions. It accomplished this with several staggeringly bold strategies—for its product, its distribution channel, and its pricing, none of which should have worked.
- **Vistaprint:** The idea for this company was hatched in an MBA course and has grown to challenge a centuries-old industry (printing), redefining how small and medium-sized businesses market themselves.
- **inVentiv Health:** Just one decade ago, inVentiv Health was battling head to head with its main competitor in an emerging type of business: providing outsourced sales and marketing services to health care companies. By 2008 the competitor's revenues had dropped by 60 percent. Meanwhile, inVentiv's revenues skyrocketed, reaching $1.1 billion by 2008, a 520 percent rise. It's a story of coordination. Through smart acquisitions, today the company encompasses a collection of distinct agencies, each with a unique capability. The magic happens when inVentiv coordinates its parts for its clients.

- **Autodesk:** Every single film that has won an Oscar for Best Visual Effects in the past 15 years has used software created by Autodesk. This is the same company that produces AutoCAD, used worldwide by architects and engineers to create three-dimensional models. Using their software capabilities to serve two very different industries was nothing short of genius.
- **Blue Nile:** This online diamond company started when a young man in search of an engagement ring tried, and failed, to get a salesperson to explain why two diamonds that looked just alike were so different in cost. Today, Blue Nile will gladly sell you a high-quality diamond, but what they really offer customers is information. With its canny strategic choices, Blue Nile was one of the few purely online businesses to survive the dot-com meltdown.
- **EyeBuyDirect:** This online retailer and optical manufacturer began in 2005 with one simple mission: to make prescription eyeglasses and other forms of vision correction affordable and accessible to everyone worldwide. By enabling rapid customization, centralizing production, and assembling a global distribution network, the company is challenging its industry's outdated structure.
- **QuEST Global:** This engineering outsourcing firm had one client when it opened its doors in 1997. As of 2011, it is surpassing $100 million in revenue, employs over 1,600 people across 17 countries, and services many of the world's largest firms. No competitors can match the close, personal, in-depth knowledge that QuEST so easily provides.
- **College Hunks Hauling Junk:** Want your junk hauled away? Call these guys, not because they'll do a good job (although they will) but because it will make you feel good. That's the premise behind the success of this company. Early on they figured out that consumers like helping college students, and now they sell the experience, not the junk-hauling expertise. They have since hit the *Inc.* 500 list of the U.S.'s fastest-growing private companies, and their $3 million revenues are still expanding.
- **Valley Forge Fabrics:** This once-small business was founded by a husband-and-wife team who had a simple idea—to sell high-quality fabrics to hotels. Over the past three decades, the company has emerged as the dominant player in its niche; it now sells more decorative upholstery fabrics to the hospitality industry than any other

company in the world. They have proved that doing good for the environment is also good for the bottom line.

- **Best Doctors:** If you have ever dreamed of transforming an industry and helping others in the process, you want to know about Best Doctors. A global provider of an innovative employee health benefit that improves the quality and cost of health care, Best Doctors has rapidly emerged as a $100 million business with the potential to grow 10 times larger.
- **Aflac:** How did a small, family-owned, run-of-the-mill insurance company from Georgia evolve into a $20 billion business with a brand icon as popular as Ronald McDonald or Mickey Mouse? Here's a hint: it's not just the duck. Actually, Aflac's success comes from the fact it invented an entirely new category of insurance.

It's obvious just from looking at the list that these companies display a very wide range of traits—different industries, products, regions, size of operation, capitalization, management structure, history, and so forth. It's what they have in common that interests us: creative leaders with bold ideas and the guts to put them into play.

> Under Heaven, there is nothing more pliant and weak than water. But for attacking the firm and strong nothing surpasses it, nothing can be exchanged for it. The weak being victorious over the strong, the pliant being victorious over the firm.
>
> —*Tao Te Ching, Chapter 78*[2]

Highly competitive companies act like water. They fill every space, seize every opportunity, and jump ahead of every trend before their competition can take action. Even as they grow, they maintain the speed and flexibility of a start-up. As a result, they expand their lead with every movement.

Winning with an Asymmetrical Playbook

To describe what these innovators do, I often use the phrase *asymmetrical playbook.* I borrowed it from the military concept of *asymmetrical warfare,* a term that describes a struggle between unequal combatants. In military usage, it implies that one of the two parties is inherently weaker—fewer troops, for instance, or poorly equipped—and compensates for that weakness with unconventional moves. The weaker troops cannot win if they do what the stronger enemy does; they must find a different approach, something smarter. Guerrilla tactics is an example.

By using the term in this book, I do not mean to suggest that the companies I profile are weak. Quite the opposite. But they do face a difficult situation and choose to attack it with a playbook that differs from their competitors'. The competitors, meanwhile, are all operating from the *same* playbook. They are so busy trying to outdo each other by performing the traditional moves better that they never see the innovators coming.

In the next five chapters, we will reveal their playbook.

CHAPTER 3

Move Early to the Next Battleground

He who is first to battle is at ease, he who is late to battle is at labor.

—Sun Tzu[1]

Traditional Playbook	New Playbook
You must win today's battleground; this positions you to win tomorrow.	You must already start moving to tomorrow's battleground; managing the *transitions* positions you to win tomorrow.

Wayne Gretzky, arguably the greatest hockey player of all time, was once asked to explain his secret. "I skate to where the puck is going to be," he said, "not where it is." Outthinkers understand that his remark is more than a sports show sound bite; it's a mind-set. And its message is simple: As the pace of change accelerates, it is not enough to have a plan to win the current game. You must simultaneously have plans for future games and know how to turn battleground shifts into an advantage.

Consider, for example, Rosetta Stone. In 2005 this innovative language software company was practically unknown; seven years later it has emerged as the world's leading provider of language learning solutions.

I had the opportunity to sit down with Rosetta Stone's chief executive officer (CEO), Tom Adams, several times. As I dug into the company's success, I found the fingerprint of an outthinker, a company that has embraced the "next battleground" mind-set and is surprising its competition by skillfully managing battleground shifts.

Plan for the Next Battle

When Adams took over in 2005, the company was selling language software in a crowded field. All the competitors' products were similar—books, tapes, and CDs designed to replace the classroom model—and all at similar price points, between $5 and $30. And Rosetta Stone, following standard business school logic, had decided to sell the first unit of their product for $20, nicely the middle of the field.

But Rosetta Stone's technology had the potential to adopt an entirely different positioning. It did not have to remain a classroom alternative. Instead, Adams explains, "We compared ourselves to the immersive experience of going to a foreign country, not being able to speak the language, and having to learn it there."[2] Adams saw a battleground shift coming down the pipeline—a transformation from classroom to immersion—and decided to take advantage of it.

To execute this strategy fully, Rosetta Stone is careful not to hire language learning experts. They do not want people who think in terms of conjugated verbs and sentence structure. Instead, Adams says, "We hire folks who are multilingual and have had the actual experience of being in another country and learning the language there. Most of them have never taught. They have practical real-world experience and they're smart."

At the same time, Adams took a hard look at his product. He realized that by approximating the competitors' pricing, they were miscategorizing their offering. If Rosetta Stone really wanted to own their positioning as a full immersion experience, they should be selling their product at a far higher price. So they immediately repackaged the product (bundling multiple $20 modules) and sold it for $300.

"Price is a proxy for quality," says Adams. "When you make a promise that people will learn and you charge $300, then you really must deliver."

Breaking into a higher price tier created a challenge: few consumers felt comfortable handing over $300 at a bookstore counter without first talking to someone about the product to learn why it was worth the cost. So Rosetta Stone had to either give up its $300 pricing strategy or diverge from industry norms. It dared to veer, in a most dramatic way.

In a move that would have most business school professors rolling their eyes, Rosetta Stone headed for the mall and airports and lined up its high-end language learning software alongside other kiosks hocking sunglasses and hair extensions. They seemed perhaps a fish out of water with their $300 software next to $20 sunglasses, but this is precisely what a smart strategist wants. The fish out of water has no other fish to contend with.

The strategy worked. Rosetta Stone's well-informed salespeople could walk customers through its unique product, addressing in full detail the concerns that stand between curiosity and purchase. These kiosks also allowed potential customers to experience the software and process that make Rosetta Stone so effective.

Now, of course, competitors are eyeing that success and making plans to copy. But Rosetta Stone is already moving on again. The battleground of the future is going to be applying social media to enhance the experience of immersion, and that is exactly what Rosetta Stone is doing.

In the second half of 2009 Rosetta Stone launched a new product called *TOTALe*. It is a combination of the Rosetta Stone core product (a series of interactive computer lessons) with two new services bolted on: a web-based, video coaching session with a live tutor and an online game room in which customers can play language games with other Rosetta Stone users.

But TOTALe has the potential to be much more because it moves the company still deeper into the next battleground. It does this in three ways. First, it moves Rosetta Stone early into social media, by linking users with other users to play language games. If you are studying Mandarin, for example, you can find another Mandarin student at your level, online anywhere in the world. The two of you can play a fun interactive game that enhances learning for both of you. If the company can start building a network effect ahead of the competition, it could build a defensible advantage.

Second, TOTALe is entirely online. No CDs or heavy programs have to be installed. As such, it steps Rosetta Stone into the software-as-service realm, or cloud computing. If we are moving to a world in which we no longer need disk drives or large hard drives because we access our applications through web browsers, as Google and increasingly Microsoft believe, then Rosetta Stone is already there.

Third, if globalization continues to drive more people to learn other languages, as Rosetta Stone is betting, the bottleneck will not be the software but rather language tutors. So as part of TOTALe, Rosetta Stone has formed an army of tutors that users can interact with via Internet video. This effectively stymies competitors: yes, a team of programmers may replicate Rosetta Stone's software, but can they assemble an army of live teachers?

Be Good

Rosetta Stone activates another strategy common to outthinkers. It's what I have called *be good*—a company mission that links financial success with social altruism. We will look at this strategy more closely in Chapter 6, illustrating the practical strategic value of pursuing a mission that benefits society. For Rosetta Stone, it is a genuinely deliberate approach.

Tom Adams explains it this way: "Basically we want to make the world a better place. We imagine a world where anyone anywhere can learn any language fluently with Rosetta Stone alone. And that will lead to a better world."

Thwart the Competition

So Rosetta Stone continually moves to the next battleground, breaking away from those who are still fighting it out on today's worn battleground. Along the way they leave behind barriers that frustrate competitors' efforts to follow: they change their hiring practices, introduce a new distribution model, build a social network of language learners, and start locking up an army of language tutors. And they pursue being good, while others choose between profit and social aims.

Competitors could conceivably overcome any one of these barriers. But Rosetta Stone complicates such efforts by weaving together their positioning with a long list of interlocking strategic decisions. If a competitor wants to copy just one element of its strategy, it must make many disruptive changes, and the cost of copying is raised exponentially.

For instance, remember Rosetta Stone's strategy of not hiring language teachers? To copy Rosetta Stone's strategy fully, any competitor would need to completely gut its workforce and hire all new employees. The cost and pain of such a transformation could postpone competitive response for some time.

Will Rosetta Stone succeed? We cannot know for sure. Leaving the pack involves immense execution risk because you must learn entirely new skills and build capabilities foreign to your core market. The boldness of its strategy separates it from the competition, but it also forces the company to stretch away from its competencies. It does seem clear that they have succeeded in blocking any competitive threats so far. To replicate Rosetta Stone's new strategy, a competitor would have to build a new service culture, social networking, and critical mass of coordinated information—and do it all before Rosetta Stone again leaps ahead.

Think Before You Shift

It's tempting to conclude that to deal with the acceleration of competition, all you have to do is get to the next battleground more quickly than your competitors. Certainly Rosetta Stone has used that strategy successfully. But the challenge of shifting battlegrounds is more complex. It's not always the first who wins. Winners are the ones who understand how to turn battleground shifts into an advantage. Sometimes that means leading. Sometimes that means following. Sometimes that means staying away from the next battleground altogether.

Sun Tzu outlines specific guidelines for when it's best to occupy a new battleground early or late. Like good generals, jazz musicians, and skilled comedians, outthinkers know the key is timing. Apple is one such player.

Looking critically at Apple's growth and success, I think I identified Apple's playbook. One of its key plays is this pattern: to catch something, you must first let it go. That approach has become part of the company's DNA.

You see, Apple is not innovative in the way most people define the term. Their brilliance comes not from introducing new cutting-edge technologies or in building new markets. Rather they let others do that work. Then Apple steps in, expands existing technology, jumps into a market space that is already growing, and uses its marketing and business-building talent to command a large share of what others have already started creating. That's exactly what happened with the iPad, a competitor to the Kindle, the Sony Reader, and Barnes & Noble's Nook.

Here Is How the Play Works

1. Someone tests out a new innovation.
2. This innovation should be attractive to consumers, but adoption is slow, either because customers do not understand the innovation or because another barrier in the overall system appears.
3. The initial innovator invests in changing the system, influencing consumer behavior, for example, and thereby initiating a battleground shift that will allow the innovation to succeed.
4. The system loosens and people start adopting the innovation.
5. Then another company (e.g., Apple), who owns critical strategic assets, steps in, draws the wind from the innovator's sails, and takes the innovation for itself.

This pattern helps explain why VHS beat out Betamax, why Gatorade has an 80 percent market share while Under Armour (which was born under nearly identical circumstances) commands only about 15 percent, and why most people say they TiVo things but they have never actually owned TiVo because they get free DVRs from their cable providers.

Apple knows when it's best to follow. It also knows when it's best to stay away from a new battleground completely. Steve Jobs famously said, "I'm as proud of what we don't do as I am of what we do."[3] Apple's soaring profits come from just a handful of products that you could fit easily on one desk: the iPhone, Mac, iPad, iPod, and revenue from iTunes and software.

Resist the Mob Mentality

As battlegrounds shift more quickly, the nature of competition changes. You must learn to effectively play through the transitions. The midsteps between games become more critical. This does not mean simply going after the next battleground first. This is not a call to just run faster. That is the obvious, overly simplistic way to compete in a complex world. Everyone will be doing that.

Winners don't do what everyone else does. They think more cleverly about how to create an advantage through a battleground shift. They know when to be first, when to follow, and when to stick to the current battleground, letting the competitors race forward like a pack of toddlers playing soccer, hovering around the ball up field, leaving the outthinkers with the field to themselves. Most important, they know how to look out across multiple games simultaneously while their competitors play myopically.

Outthinkers also know how to hold back a battleground shift. When you are winning on today's battleground, you may be better off slowing the shift to a new one. This takes skill. The story of the incumbent who holds on too long, grows rigid, and falls has become a cliché. But if you maintain your connection to reality and are able to honestly assess whether time is on your side, you can create an enormous advantage.

Conclusion

In the old view of the world, we worried about winning on today's battlefield, mostly hoping that success today would automatically lead to success tomorrow. This worked when battlefields tended to stay the same. But battlefields are now shifting rapidly, making it important to pay attention to multiple challenges simultaneously and to get comfortable with multiple simultaneous strategies.

The willingness to play for today and tomorrow *at the same time* is a distinguishing characteristic of innovators. Think of golfers, who practice both their long game and their short game because they must shift between the two during a tournament. Or consider chess players, who see 10 moves ahead and then choose one.

Companies that cannot see both plays simultaneously usually make a serious error when trouble develops. They shift their focus to immediate tactics needed to survive today's problems, which only damages their chances of winning tomorrow. Rather than prevent defeat, they have only postponed it.

CHAPTER 4

Coordinate the Uncoordinated

With formation, the army achieves victories yet they do not understand how. Everyone knows the formation by which you achieved victory, yet no one knows the formations by which you were able to create victory. Therefore, your strategy for victories in battle is not repetitious, and your formations in response to the enemy are endless.

—Sun Tzu[1]

Traditional Playbook	New Playbook
You create power by owning things and keeping them inside your walls.	You can create power by coordinating things, often indirectly, outside your walls.

However else history may judge Napoleon Bonaparte, he was indisputably a military genius. He created a new form of battle that totally baffled his enemies; a technique he called *maneuvre sur les derrieres,* or *maneuver at the rear.* Bonaparte broke his army into separate columns, each threatening a different target. His opponent had to disperse its forces to defend multiple locations. Suddenly Bonaparte's swarm of columns would shift direction mid-path, concentrating their force on one common target and overwhelming the enemy now spread too thin to defend itself.

This is the power of coordination. It is a lesson outthinkers are applying today on the corporate battlefield.

What has changed since Bonaparte's time is not that coordination creates power—the ability to coordinate has always been the source of power. What has changed is *how* we create power. While competitors remain rooted in an outdated model that holds that we must own things to exert power, today's outthinkers see they can increasingly build power without ownership. Adopt this mind-set and you have a chance to compete on tomorrow's battlefield.

Revolutions and Coordination

The most dramatic evidence of the shift from ownership to coordination came in 2011 in the Middle East. We saw entrenched autocrats suddenly fall in Tunisia, Egypt, and across the region. Why did this happen in 2011 and not five years earlier? Because advances in technology and the broad acceptance of social media had created a level of connectivity unimagined just a few years ago. That connectivity is fundamentally changing society by enhancing our ability to coordinate. This mammoth change has four ingredients: speed, syndication, integrity, and transparency.

Speed

When Paul Revere made his now famous horseback ride, shouting, "The British are coming!" to rally American patriots, his 13.5-mile trip took at least 2 hours. In a modern car, he could have made the trip in 45 minutes. With a telephone he could have spread the word in about 15 minutes. Today, one tweet or a Facebook update could do the job in 3 seconds. Think about that. The time for a revolutionary community to react to a threat has shrunk from 2 hours to 3 seconds.

Syndication

If Revere's message ended up reaching the wrong person, such as someone who didn't care or, worse yet, someone who disagreed with him (a British loyalist, for example), the movement might never have built momentum. This is like placing dominoes too far apart from each other. You push one, but because it cannot reach its neighbor, it falls short, causing no chain reaction. Ancient Rome survived multiple attempted revolutions in the first century BC, in part by preventing would-be revolutionaries from connecting with each other.

Today technology not only allows you to transmit your message more quickly, it also allows you to syndicate it more broadly so that you can reach the people who agree with and will take action with you. The chances of your revolution's petering out dramatically diminish.

Integrity

You probably played the telephone chain game as a child. You whisper a message to the person standing next to you. That person whispers the same message to his or her neighbor, and so on. By the time the message travels around the circle, it sounds nothing like the one you started. Message integrity is reduced with each transmission. Today, it is easier for your friends to share your message exactly as you wrote it, quickly to a large group of people. With fewer communication errors you can share more detailed messages.

At an American Eagle Outfitters store around the corner from my office in New York, for example, store workers were shocked to find hundreds of pedestrians suddenly taking off their shirts and walking by at precisely the same time. They could do this because their message—probably something like, "Walk in front of American Eagle Outfitters on Wednesday at 3:32 PM and take off your shirt"—was spread without distortion.

Transparency

Machiavelli pointed to the greatest barrier to revolutionary movements when he wrote,

> *And it will always happen that he who is not your friend will request your neutrality and he who is your friend will ask you to declare yourself by taking up arms. And irresolute princes, in order to avoid present dangers, follow the neutral road most of the time, and most of the time they are ruined.*[2]

Most people choose the neutral road. Only a few are willing to take up arms. In the same way, most customers choose to stick with neutral technology and only a few—the early adopters—are willing to take up the new thing.

Dictators (and powerful incumbent corporations) depend on this dynamic to hold on to power. By quelling unrest early, they preempt even the appearance that unrest exists. People think, "This government, this leader, is not working for me," but they look around and think they are in the small minority, so they put up with it. Consumers think, "I really don't like this product," but everyone they speak to seems to be using it, so they go along.

Today, it is easier than ever to express our discontent. We can do it anonymously, so it is safe, and we can more easily find supporters. We discover more quickly that we are not alone. The leap—or the *chasm* as author Geoffrey A. Moore calls it in his classic *Crossing the Chasm*—between your revolution's early adopters and the early majority is collapsing.

The shrinking of these four barriers is fundamentally changing our ability to organize ourselves. We can send messages more quickly (speed), multiply our odds of reaching the right people (syndication), more easily transmit our message without distortion (integrity), and show the world they are not alone (transparency). Just as the disappearance of these barriers has transformed the political map of the Middle East, it is also transforming the power dynamic of industries. Take, for example, the pharmaceutical industry.

Playing with the Pieces: inVentiv Health

Businesses around the world are falling apart, so to speak. Over the past 15 years, technology has dramatically cut the costs of coordination, meaning things that corporations once had to manage internally can now be outsourced (that is, they can pay someone else to do them). The first wave hit the obvious functions, things like information technology (IT) support and call center management that were labor-intensive and could be remotely performed. But the frontline of outsourcing is continually expanding to higher-end functions. It is becoming increasingly attractive, for example, to outsource high-end research and development (as QuEST, another company we will discuss later, shows) or high-skilled sales.

So when one of my clients, a medical device company, decided to take a fresh look at how they organize their sales force, we wanted to at least consider some kind of outsourcing option. And we started with the largest: inVentiv Health.

In 2002 inVentiv Health and PDI Inc. were battling head-to-head in an emerging business model. Pharmaceutical firms were beginning to look seriously at their variable cost structure and flexibility, looking for partners who perform noncore, nonstrategic activities at a lower cost than they could on their own.

inVentiv and PDI both seemed well positioned to ride the coming wave. Each was standing at about $250 million in revenue and eager to grow. But they would pursue growth through very distinct strategies. Over the next seven years, PDI's revenues steadily slipped, falling to just $115 million by 2008, a 60 percent drop. Meanwhile inVentiv's revenues skyrocketed, reaching $1.1 billion by 2008, a 520 percent rise.

How did two companies so alike in size and ambition design for themselves such divergent futures? I had the chance to talk at length with both chief executive officers (CEOs). Although many subtle differences in strategy can explain the radically divergent trajectories, the core difference is that inVentiv embraced the "coordinate the uncoordinated" mind-set, whereas PDI held more closely to the traditional view.

Coordinate the Uncoordinated

inVentiv understands that power comes from coordination. It is strategically acquiring new firms to form a comprehensive set of services so that it can fill any gap that a pharmaceutical firm may want to outsource. Today, the company encompasses a diverse constellation of companies, from a research firm to a marketing agency, each with a unique capability but all specialized in pharmaceuticals. They can conduct pharmaceutical R&D, they can build new product launches, and they can turn on a sales force. Across almost every step in the chain, inVentiv has a company that can help you.

Another one of my clients was looking to commercialize an innovative treatment for acquired immunodeficiency syndrome (AIDS) in the United States. We found that were we to hire inVentiv, we could practically check off boxes and outsource any piece of the business we did not want to build ourselves. R&D? Check. Pursuing U.S. Food and Drug Administration (FDA) approval? Check. Building a nationwide sales force? Just turn on the inVentiv sales force. The company is a coordination machine. The coordination that pharmaceutical companies achieve through internal divisions and reporting structure, inVentiv achieves through the coordination of semi-autonomous firms.

Move Early to the Next Battleground

When we look at inVentiv, we see only characteristics of today's outthinkers. For example, inVentiv is guided by the future, the next battleground. They're not content to merely fight today's battle, like their competitors; they simultaneously look at tomorrow's.

As inVentiv's CEO, Blane Walter, explained to me, "The pharma and healthcare model is changing. Payers have a growing influence, and as a result, you need to appeal to all stakeholders. So we started two or three ago working on delivering integrated services. Now 15-20 percent of our revenue comes from integrated services. It was less than 5 percent a few years ago."[3]

By fully executing just these two strategies—coordinating the uncoordinated and moving early to the next battleground—inVentiv has quickly slipped in front of a thunderous wave that promises to transform the pharmaceutical industry. Since I began researching the company, it was brought private by a private equity firm and is gearing up to further accelerate its attack.

Coordinating Beyond Facebook

When we seek to explain events or businesses that take advantage of this shift toward coordinating the uncoordinated, it is tempting to grow too enthralled with Facebook, Twitter, LinkedIn, and their peers. To do this is to risk missing out on some other exciting, and potentially more promising, emerging companies. These are companies that deliberately stay away from the glamor of social media because they are focused on transforming the darker corners of the economy.

Consider, for example, FedBid, which is helping governments reinvent how they buy things. The company enables federal agencies to procure products and commodities through a full-service online marketplace using a reverse auction process in which vendors vie to provide the government with what it needs.

Let's say you are a buyer supporting government research scientists, and they need 20 ferrets for an experiment. FedBid helps you go online, quickly specify your acquisition scenario, describe your requirements, and post your buy onto the marketplace. FedBid notifies qualified ferret providers, who compete to provide you with what you need at the best value—not only the best price but also the exact ferrets you need when you need them.

The amount of goods sold through reverse auctions has grown by more than 50 percent between 2008 and 2010, and FedBid is helping lead this growth. Government agencies purchased $1.15 billion worth of products and commodities through the company's online marketplace in 2010. FedBid's president, Glenn Richardson, is a good friend of mine. A former military man and a partner in several large consulting firms, Richardson was drawn to FedBid's promise. "We are truly a game changer," he explains. "By improving the competitive process, we have been able to maximize the value of every tax dollar used to make purchases through FedBid."[4] He sees that the lowering cost of coordination must inevitably transform how the government operates and is racing to position FedBid ahead of the coming wave.

Rave Mobile Safety is another example of a company seizing the coordination trend from beyond the spotlight and solving a huge community problem in the process. Dial 911 from your home phone, and the police will know your precise address. But dial it from your mobile phone, and the dispatcher has very little idea where you are. Since mobile phone penetration in the United States is greater than 75 percent, and is greater than 100 percent in Western Europe, Japan, and Hong Kong, this is a problem.

Luckily, some smart people are already addressing the issue. Rave Mobile Safety, for example, started off helping universities broadcast messages to their students. If classes are canceled tomorrow because of a snowstorm, a university can send out an e-mail and text message immediately to all students' mobile phones, regardless of what carrier they use. But Rave Mobile soon found copycat competitors encroaching on their turf.

So the company stepped back and asked itself, "What assets could we leverage to pursue a truly disruptive opportunity?" They recognized their power came not from their technology (although they own lots of patents) but from their ability to coordinate three key communities: service providers (Rave Mobile has assembled relationships with every major mobile phone carrier), 911 operators (many of Rave Mobile's university clients also operate their towns' 911 centers), and citizens.

Rave Mobile Safety is now building a nationwide database of voluntarily provided information from mobile phone users throughout the country. If you sign up for Rave Mobile Safety service, which is free, you will be invited to share the information you would want a 911 operator to know about you in the case of an emergency. Your name and home address would be added, of course. But it might also be useful for them to know the names of your spouse or your children, what medicines you are allergic to, and any health conditions you have. The endgame that Rave Mobile Safety appears to be playing is the creation of the definitive database for 911 services.

Neither company is alone; both have competitors. But FedBid and Rave Mobile are ahead of a transformative wave, and if they make the right moves, they could follow a path similar to that of Google or Microsoft in developing and owning a critical piece to a puzzle of worldwide significance.

Coordinating Air Travel

If you've never made the flight to Bentonville, Arkansas, you are missing something extraordinary. The smallness of your plane and the vista of an endless patchwork of farmland connected by country roads hide the fact that you are entering Walmart country. The passengers to your right and left, now fumbling with their seat belts and grabbing warm coats, fall into one of two categories. They are either there to pitch something to the world's largest retailer, silently rehearsing their negotiation pitch, or they are there to extract the greatest value for their company and their loyal Walmart customers.

When Peter H. Leiman and Cameron Odgen, two Harvard Business School MBA students, made the trip, they were probably rehearsing their lines. They were there to pitch a proof of concept that they had been working on in school, an idea that could save Walmart 25 percent on its airline travel expenses. The pitch was simple: if Walmart used small, inexpensive jets to shuttle its people around, and filled each jet with four people, it could travel with greater flexibility at a lower cost.

The pitch worked, but not in the direction you might expect. It served to convince these two young entrepreneurs that, even though they had no real business-building experience, they should start an airline. They have since raised $30 million and launched Europe's first air taxi company, Blink, based in London with hubs in Geneva and the Channel Islands. Their vision: to redefine the world of short-haul travel.

I had a chance to interview Leiman and Blink's chief information officer, Jake Peters. As they laid out their strategy and business model, I caught clear signs that they are adopting to coordinate the uncoordinated mind-set. Their vision for the future of air travel is that airplanes will become taxis instead of buses. Instead of lining up to board one plane with a hundred others going somewhere in your general direction, you will book an airplane that fits just a few people, that is ready to go precisely where you want to go.

Although this model lacks the scale efficiency of funneling lots of passengers onto big planes, it has the potential of making up for this by seizing what in our interview we termed *economies of serendipity*. When enough air taxis are circulating, there is a good chance that the plane bringing you to your destination will have another group waiting there to take the same plane back. Coordinating small groups of passengers, rather than herding hundreds around, is becoming more efficient.

Leiman and Peters make thousands of strategic choices that seem obvious from their perspective but that would seem crazy from the perspective of a traditional airline. It is these thousands of small decisions—from how they recruit and train to what type of seats to install in planes—that weave a web of advantages that competitors have trouble replicating.

Internal Coordination

Not only is the power of coordination growing externally (as Wikipedia, Facebook, FedBid, and Rave Mobile show), its importance is also expanding inside the corporate walls. The same trends—new technology, new mind-sets, and new social norms—that are enabling us to coordinate elements in our environments are enabling us to better coordinate internally. Companies that are winning are embracing these changes.

When Akio Morita, Sony's founder, strolled through his labs and saw engineers working with small speakers attached their heads to listen to music privately, he made a connection. In another lab he remembered seeing a different group of engineers working on a portable tape player. He observed and oriented (put two pieces of information together) and came up with a new idea: a portable, personal music player. The Walkman revolutionized the electronics industry and created the concept of mobile music.

We are seeing a plethora of new companies emerging that are helping businesses accelerate the coordination process that Morita facilitated inside Sony.

Attivio, for example, is using what it calls *Unified Information Access (UIA)* to bring this cross-pollination and coordination to an entire company electronically. It essentially takes the structured dashboards and reports of business intelligence and mashes them together with Google-esque unstructured search results to give you all the information that is relevant to you in one place, regardless of where the information comes from.

For instance, if your company serves Coca-Cola, and Coca-Cola makes a payment on an invoice, then not only would the accounts receivable department know about the payment, but that information would also find its way to the account representative responsible for managing the Coca-Cola relationship. He gets this information because he set up a query for information about anything having to do with Coca-Cola.

It looks like Attivio has the right idea. It grew 300 percent last year and doubled its client base, attracting some big new names, including Advance Micro Devices (AMD). AMD said they went with Attivio because "we needed a new approach to information access that extended beyond traditional search capabilities."[5]

Conclusion

The nature of power has not changed. Power always depended on our ability to coordinate things. What is changing is *how* we coordinate. It is less important to own and control things because new technologies, mind-sets, and behavior patterns are opening up an entirely new mode to consider. New opportunities exist outside and inside our organizations.

CHAPTER 5

Force Two-Front Battles

Appear at places where he must rush to defend, and rush to places where he least expects.

—Sun Tzu[1]

Traditional Playbook	New Playbook
We are experts in our industry, so we will compete within industry lines. This leads to single-front battles.	Our expertise is unrelated to our industry, so we will leverage our expertise across industry boundaries. This forces competitors onto two-front battles.

One of the greatest Union generals in the American Civil War, William Tecumseh Sherman, once said that the goal of effective military strategy was to maneuver so that the opposing general finds himself or herself *on the horns of a dilemma*. He meant forcing the enemy into the impossible position of having to defend one target by sacrificing another.

General Sherman applied this strategy repeatedly throughout the Carolinas and Georgia between 1864 and 1865. He would separate his troops into two or more distant columns, each threatening a different target. This prevented his opponents from concentrating their forces against him. Now forced to break up and defend multiple apparent targets, his opponents found they lacked the mass to defend any single target.

The principle Sherman implemented has ancient roots. Chinese military strategists advocated it over 3,000 years ago and I got a chance to connect to that history during a recent visit to the Shanghai Museum. Strolling through a dimly lit room surrounded by sculptures and bronzes, many more than 1,500 years old, I saw three names repeated: Wei, Zhao, and Chi. These are the three states that played out a famous Chinese story from which this two-front battle strategy originates.

Zhao was preparing for an attack by Wei and worried the state would not be able to survive; the leaders asked a neighboring state, Chi, for help. Chi agreed and prepared its soldiers for battle. But at the last minute, just before Chi's forces began their march to save their ally, an advisor suggested a different, counterintuitive strategy. Rather than help defend Zhao, he argued, Chi should attack the aggressor. This would force Wei's troops into a dilemma: Should they continue their march toward Zhao and secure what seemed a likely victory, or should they return home to save the women and children they had left poorly defended? Wei would inevitably return home. By forcing Wei into this dilemma, Chi saved its ally and defeated its enemy in one swift move.

This is not unlike the dilemma the Army football team mentioned in Chapter 1 faced: their players could either rush toward the ball, in which case Notre Dame would pass the ball down the field, or they could fall back to intercept the pass, in which case Notre Dame would run the ball through the now-empty defensive line.

What these two strategies have in common is that the outthinker forces its competitor onto a two-front battle. On the horns of a dilemma, they can either run to protect themselves against one end of the horn, while exposing themselves to the other, or vice versa, but they cannot do both.

Today's business outthinkers are using this strategy to great effect, and they start by ignoring the idea that we should define a business by the industry it occupies. Because they do not limit their focus within accepted industry bounds, they compete across multiple market fronts. They use one business to create cover for another, forcing competitors to battle unexpected rivals from seemingly unrelated domains.

Consider Autodesk the maker of AutoCAD, a powerful software program used by engineers and architects to build three-dimensional (3D) computer models. When Autodesk looked for new growth possibilities, they discovered a very untraditional opportunity. They realized they could focus their decades of experience with digital 3D on an unsuspecting competitor: video animators. So Autodesk created a new version of its software to be used for film animation, a new program they called *Maya.* Over the past 15 years, Maya has been used by every film that has won Best Visual Effects at the Academy Awards. The chief executive officer (CEO) of an animation company based in the Philippines told me that Maya now has, by his estimation, a 60 percent market share.

What makes Maya so successful is that it enjoys coverage from Autodesk's core product, AutoCAD. The young techies who flocked to video companies because they wanted to work on advancing the technology never expected to be attacked by an architectural software company. They never planned to have to compete with a company that leveraged 30 years of 3D imaging experience. This may be one reason Autodesk's stock price has grown from $15 to more than $40 over the past five years.

This strategic pattern—forcing the competitor into a defensive position by flustering them with a two-front battle—lies at the heart of many outthinker successes. In business as in war, the key elements of the strategy are the same:

- You launch a second attack simultaneously with the first.
- This forces your competitor to defend against that second attack.
- In defending itself, the competitor makes itself vulnerable to the first attack or, at least, takes a passive posture.
- You advance with relative ease.

The reason outthinkers are able to apply this pattern so fluidly is that they do not define their boundaries by their industry. By projecting from a stronghold unrelated to industry, they can surgically target opportunities across sectors. Sometimes this means they operate in areas that seem so unrelated that only someone who really understands the company's core strength can discern the strategic logic. But launching a two-front battle need not take you far from your core. Consider the *Wall Street Journal*.

■ ■ ■

It takes about 40 minutes by train to get from my home into New York City, just enough time to get through the *Wall Street Journal* and knock off a few morning e-mails. But last month I left my e-mails untouched and instead enjoyed a special treat: the *Journal*'s New York section, dedicated to covering New York's local political, real estate, and entertainment news. On the surface, this may seem like just a product expansion, but it illustrates a powerful strategic pattern. As it turns out, a former business classmate of mine is now the *Wall Street Journal*'s general manager, so I got some firsthand insight into what is going on.

For years the *New York Times* has been slowly abandoning its New York stronghold in pursuit of the national, and international, market. And the *Journal* noticed. As my friend said, "When we started exploring the opportunity, we found that in the past decade the *Times* had seen a nearly 40 percent decline in its circulation in the New York market."[2]

So, the *Journal* decided to move in. New York advertisers are hungry for a platform to put their ads in front of New York readers. Why should they pay for the eyeballs the *Times* attracts from across the country and the world when they are selling shoes on Madison Avenue? By creating a separate section of exclusively local content, the *Journal* offers advertisers a targeted vehicle to advertise to commuters like me, who may actually decide to stop by that Madison Avenue store today.

But the deeper value of this strategy is that it forces the *Times* into a defensive position. Now they have to choose between continuing their strategy of becoming a national, or even international, newspaper or retreating back to being a local paper. The *Times* is finding itself torn between two inconsistent choices, and while it untangles this conflict, while it plans and strategizes, the *Wall Street Journal* grows.

■ ■ ■

Diamond retailer Blue Nile is another outthinker that has reaped the benefits of implementing this strategy.

In the late 1990s, a young man named Mark Vadon was looking for an engagement ring. Like millions of other men who face one of the most important purchases of their lives with no experience to refer to, he felt confused. "One ring was $12,000, one was $17,000. I said, that's more than my car cost, and I can't tell the difference. So I asked [the salesman] and he told me to pick the ring that 'speaks' to me. I thought that was bullshit."[3]

Vadon's journey eventually led him to not only a new wife but also an unlikely new profession: he became a diamond salesman himself. In 1999, he bought a diamond store and launched Blue Nile as an online diamond retailer, just as the dot-com bubble was bursting. Blue Nile was one of the few pure online businesses to survive. In its first four years it grew to $120 million in revenue. In 2003 it went public, and over the next five years, it expanded 250 percent, reaching $320 million in annual revenue.[4]

We cannot explain Blue Nile's success with traditional logic. They own no diamond mines, as De Beers does. They can claim no scale advantages. And unlike Tiffany's, they enjoyed no preexisting customer captivity. But if we look closely, we see the mind of an outthinker at work.

Selling Information, Not Diamonds

Blue Nile's divergence from industry standards begins with its purpose. Most jewelers exist for the jewelry. By contrast Blue Nile's CEO describes her company's purpose this way: "Our focus is empowering the customer with information."[5] The average customer looks at more than 200 pages of information, spends more than three weeks on the Blue

Nile site, and calls Blue Nile's customer service line in Seattle to talk things through with a live person. If you cannot imagine a Tiffany's salesperson cheerfully greeting a customer who has been popping in for the past three weeks and walking that customer through 200 pages of information, then you begin to see the disruptive power of Blue Nile's focus.

The Two-Horn Dilemma

Much of Blue Nile's success comes from the two-front battle strategy. To see this, imagine you are the CEO of a traditional diamond retailer trying to compete with Blue Nile. You know Blue Nile is growing and is more profitable, in percentage terms, than you are. You have resources and a brand so you figure you should simply copy Blue Nile's model of selling high-quality diamonds online. But as you think through your strategy, you find yourself practically paralyzed by the tough choices.

You could sell low-cost diamonds online. But this would not compete with Blue Nile's high-quality strategy. Blue Nile would keep picking off your high-end customers.

Or you could offer high-end diamonds online, the same quality as in your store but at a lower price because you don't have the same overhead. But that will just send a message that your in-store product is overpriced. Now you have to ask yourself: Do I sell cheap diamonds online, or do I abandon any serious efforts to sell diamonds online? Blue Nile, incidentally, does not care which you do because in either case, you are choosing not to compete with them.

But, as we know from Chapter 3, innovators must contend not just with existing competitors; they must also prepare themselves for future ones. An analysis of Blue Nile's strategy shows it is building an additional competitive shield that, if skillfully assembled, could deflect would-be attackers for a considerable amount of time.

Blue Nile also implements another outthinker strategy: it coordinates the uncoordinated (see Chapter 4) by building a global network of diamond suppliers who, because they are plugged into Blue Nile's system, make their inventory immediately visible to online shoppers. Here's how it works: When online shoppers choose a diamond, they also pick a particular style—the mounting, the ring size, the ring design, the material, and so forth. Once the shopper purchases the ring, Blue Nile's system immediately swings into action. The diamond is shipped from the supplier to Blue Nile's design center, where a designer builds the ring and mounts the diamond to the customer's specifications. And then finally the complete, customized diamond ring is mailed to the customer.

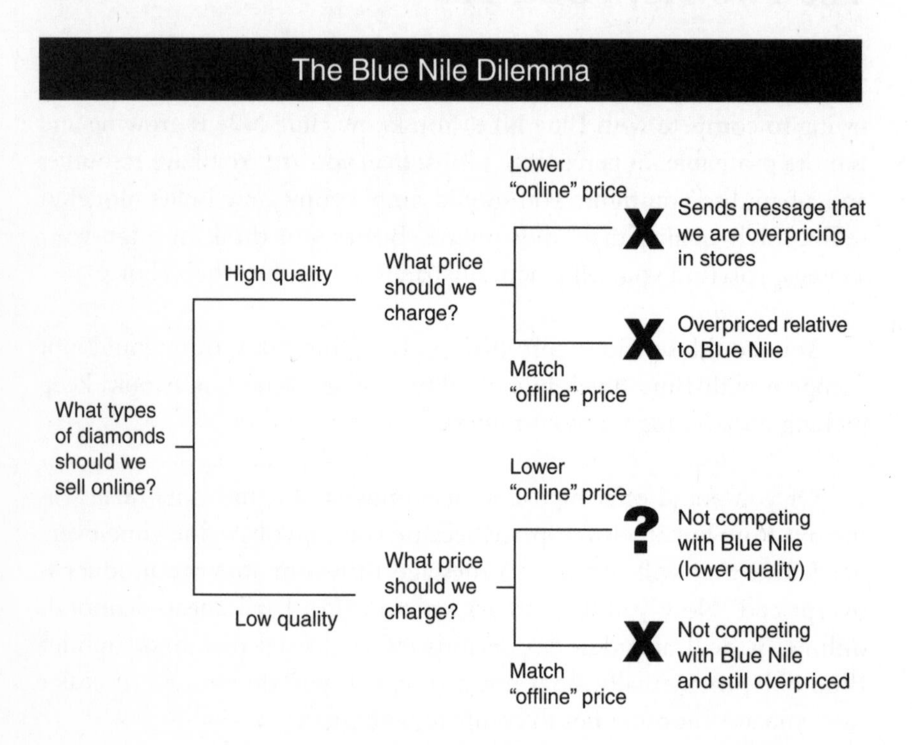

By being the first to coordinate major diamond suppliers, online, at such a scale, Blue Nile can demand exclusivity of its suppliers. "It's not like we have 10 green T-shirts and we sell them and then we order 10 more," explains CEO Diane Irvine. "Every diamond we've ever sold is unique. No one else can do that."[6]

Blue Nile's competitors may have trouble catching up to their strategy, but outthinkers in other industries are finding success the same way. Roy Hessel heads an innovative online retailer called *EyeBuyDirect* that is subjecting the eyeglass industry to the same disruptive treatment. The company has been growing at a mind-boggling rate; they ship around the world and operate several eyeglass partnerships.

■ ■ ■

Another outthinker that seems to be using this strategy effectively is QuEST, a rapidly growing provider of outsourced research and development services. It has grown revenue to nearly $120 million in 2011, from about $20 million five years ago.

Although most of his friends applied to master's programs in India, Ajit Prabhu, now CEO of QuEST Global, set his postgraduate ambitions on the United States. After earning a couple of engineering degrees, Prabhu took a job in R&D for General Electric. "I did not know how big GE was in 1997," he says now. "I thought they only made lightbulbs."[7]

Although Prabhu enjoyed his work at General Electric (GE), he could not suppress his desire to start a business. He noticed that his boss continually struggled with retaining enough engineering staff and was forced to rely on relatively small local employment agencies and consultancies. But more often than not, the applicants didn't actually meet the company's needs. Over and over, Prabhu heard the managers complain about having to sift through piles of applications to find only one or two people who actually fit the job requirements.

An entrepreneur at heart, Prabhu could not resist what he saw as an exciting opportunity. The result was QuEST, which provides engineering R&D talent to U.S. companies with a unique format he calls the *global-local* model.

The typical QuEST project involves two phases. First, a QuEST engineer is assigned to meet with the client. This face-to-face contact lowers the risk of miscommunication, allows the QuEST engineer to collaborate more efficiently with the client's engineers, and helps provide an understanding of the cultural context for the work. Then the engineering work that produces the solution is done by QuEST engineers in India.

QuEST's model is designed to optimize the workload by providing the collaborative client-facing work locally, and then produce the problem solving abroad. This approach seems simple, but it puts competitors right into a two-front dilemma. Most competitors conceive themselves as either local, high-value engineering firms or as low-cost, foreign outsourcing firms. Although their websites may claim otherwise, a dissection of their organizational and incentive structure clearly places them as *either* local or global, but not both. QuEST, by contrast, conceived itself from the beginning as being neither an Indian firm nor a U.S. firm, but both. "You have to find a global optimum. That's not in one location,"[8] says Prabhu.

It may appear unorthodox to some, but this model seems to be working. Today, a significant portion of QuEST's business comes from a few deep, strategic relationships, including Pratt & Whitney (150 engineers), Rolls-Royce (300 engineers), Toshiba (50 engineers), Procter & Gamble (30 engineers), and, of course, GE (350 engineers). These relationships provide QuEST with an unparalleled strategic advantage.

More important, QuEST's management has designed its entire business around this unique concept. As a result, they have strung together a sequence of interlocking decisions in such a way that competitors cannot easily copy them. As Prabhu says, "Our strategy is something that is easy for others to understand, but hard for someone to duplicate."[9]

■ ■ ■

When Omar Soliman and Nick Friedman, recent college grads, started collecting unwanted junk, they were out to build an empire. But two years later their business was struggling. So they sat down with entrepreneurship guru Michael Gerber, and the result of that conversation turned them instantly onto a new growth path. They have since hit the *Inc.* 500 list of the U.S.'s fastest-growing private companies, and their $3 million revenues are still expanding.

What insight did their meeting with Gerber reveal? It pointed them in the direction of the two-front battle strategy.

When Gerber asked them, "Why do people like to do business with you?" the team realized it had nothing to do with their garbage-removal expertise. It was because people have fond memories of their college days, and they like helping college students. When they hire College Hunks Hauling Junk, they don't just expect their garbage to be removed, they expect an experience, a connection to earlier, more carefree days.

That one insight shifted their company's identity—they would now operate like a university. Suddenly they made a number of small business decisions that seem counterintuitive for a regular junk-removal company. Their untraditional strategy has flustered competitors by forcing them to choose between making painful changes to their operations model or to just let College Hunks grow.

Conclusion

By engaging two battlefronts at once, and by executing cleverly on both, outthinkers are throwing their competitors into a frustrating, paralyzing dilemma. While the competitors dither about which angle to combat, the outthinkers are already moving forward to the future.

CHAPTER 6

Be Good

If we could reduce deaths from even one disease, like ovarian cancer, the return on investment would be priceless.

—Michael Milken[1]

He who exercises government by means of his virtue may be compared to the north polar star, which keeps its place and all the stars turn towards it.

—Confucius, The Analects[2]

Traditional Playbook	New Playbook
Corporations exist to serve shareholders and, secondarily, customers.	Corporations are better off serving all stakeholders: shareholders, customers, employees, the community, the country, and the environment/world.

There is a shift under way from making money to doing good. Ironically, the two have always been the same, but we haven't always been able to see it. Call it what you will—social enterprise, Karma capital, or the triple bottom line—but the trend is real, and it is rooted in both modern science and proven strategic logic. The simple fact is, doing good makes you money.

In 1990, when I was in business school at Wharton, I had a dorm-mate who loved to shout out the famous line from the original *Wall Street* movie: "Greed is good. Greed works." In fact, this greed is good culture pervaded business schools and business literature throughout most of that decade and the next, proclaiming the message that companies exist to serve shareholders and make as much money for them as possible. As a waiter during college, I was told the customer is always right. And in my classrooms, I was told that for companies the shareholder is always right.

But this view is changing. The collapse of Enron followed by a domino chain of other high-profile failures awoke investors, managers, employees, and society to the realization that something is missing.

What we see today is that the companies who are winning have moved beyond the old model. They recognize that being good has strategic, measurable value, not just to investors and customers but also to employees, their communities, their countries, society, and the environment.

Walmart, for example, built such resistance for its stores that it had to pull an embarrassing about-face and leave its stores in Europe. In the United States, efforts to build stores consistently triggered community protests and legislative hurdles. Eventually, though, they got it. Walmart began to understand what Taoist philosophers have preached for millennia: if you push, you create resistance.

Walmart started with simple changes, like promoting energy-conserving lightbulbs and reducing packaging waste. Then it began adjusting its people policies, and it started seeing results. Growth in the United States improved, and in places like Mexico, Walmart became the good guy, protecting consumers against a retail oligopoly. Today, the company continues to expand, adopting a strategy geared toward showing it benefits employees and the communities it serves.

In regions in which Walmart has operated for a long time, it still struggles against community resistance, the result of years of operating under the old model. Walmart has been trying unsuccessfully to set up small-format city stores in New York for years now. But their efforts ignite heated opposition from unions and local politicians. Meanwhile, the German giant Aldi (the sixth largest retailer in the world) has been opening up small-format urban stores throughout the United States. It uses a plethora of disruptive strategies (explored more in Chapter 18), bolstered with a robust social strategy. Aldi takes times to build local support, usually getting space from a small, local landlord who has strong community connections. It helps that the company is relatively unknown in the United States, so its actions don't attract automatic attention. And Aldi is growing. As of 2009, it generated an estimated $6 billion in revenue from the United States.[3]

Being Good Builds Moral Force

The strategic rationale for being good actually has ancient military roots. Carl von Clausewitz, the great nineteenth-century Prussian military strategist, introduced us to the concept of *moral force*. He believed that, in addition to physical force, the best armies also have equally important spiritual and moral forces, such as dedication and a sense of sacrifice. When physical strength is not enough to win, moral force can carry the soldiers to victory.

This same moral force is the fuel that drives the success of many of the outthinkers we cover here. They are pursuing a bigger goal, one that appeals to a larger class of stakeholders: the community, the country, and the world. Everyone, as a result, is cheering for them to win. If he were alive today, von Clausewitz would surely approve; he might even enjoy a certain football game.

■ ■ ■

In the 2010 Super Bowl game, the New Orleans Saints were playing for more than their team; they were playing for their city, the beautiful city that just four and a half years earlier had been devastated by Hurricane Katrina. The city the U.S. government had failed to lift up out of the floods was lifting itself up. This journey was exemplified by the Saints, a football team that since its founding in 1967 had never made it to the Super Bowl.

As the game day approached, we heard Saints players using words like *destiny* and *true calling*. Even in New York, when I had bumped into friends on the streets, our conversations usually turned to the game. When they asked who I was cheering for, I would tell them the Saints, and then I would tell them why: my wife, who grew up in New Orleans and whose family survived Katrina, has wished for this her whole life. Invariably the friends would pause and then say, "That's great, man. No one deserves it more than them."

■ ■ ■

Being good is not a fad, and it's not eye-rolling pop psychology. It is fundamental to human nature, as recent research reveals. Dr. Marco Iacoboni is a UCLA neurologist and neuroscientist and author of *Mirroring People: The New Science of How We Connect with Others*. He is a leading authority on mirror neurons, a recently discovered phenomenon that some experts predict will transform neuroscience just as the discovery of DNA transformed biology. Iacoboni believes that mirror neurons show that human beings are wired to be empathetic and good.

As he explained to me, "Overall, every human is similar. If I see someone smiling, then I smile. If I see someone crying, then I know exactly what they are going through because my mirror neurons are firing in my brain as if I am actually smiling or crying."[4]

It is the immediacy of the emotional connection between people that makes mirror neurons so intriguing. Iacoboni performed a fascinating experiment. He and his colleagues showed people—a mix of Democrats and Republicans—photographs of candidates during the 2004 election. When people saw an image of a politician in their own party, their mirror neurons fired strongly, showing an immediate feeling of empathy. When those same people recognized the image of someone in the opposite party, a remarkable sequence of activity was triggered. First their mirror neurons fired, indicating a natural empathy. Then their logical conscious mind kicked in and suppressed the mirror neurons.

The implication of this sequence is significant. It means that people's natural impulse—your customers, employees, politicians, community members, and so on—is to empathize with your cause. It is only after they recognize who you are or what your brand stands for that they may want to resist you. By developing a brand that evokes mirror neurons, by being good, you can more easily build support for your cause.

Building Followership by Being Good

Things won are done, joy's soul lies in the doing.

—*William Shakespeare*[5]

I was in Bangladesh, staring out my car window at the frenetic street pace, when I saw a crowd slowly strolling behind a white-haired, dreadlocked man. He may be, it turns out, the Forrest Gump of South Asia.

He marches every day. He never speaks, and thus he has never explained his purpose, so people have simply made up the purpose themselves. They say he is a saint. They believe following him will bring good luck. Every morning he collects a crowd that flocks around him as he circles city blocks all day.

He could be marching for any number of reasons, rational or otherwise. The facts do not point us to a clear answer, so the human desire for purpose steps in. Within the story of this man lies a lesson on leadership: Leaders create meaning not only by passionately evoking a vision but by filling a gap their people need to have filled. They provide hope where people cannot find it.

A leader is a dealer in hope.

—*Napoleon Bonaparte*[6]

My colleagues at BlessingWhite teach thousands of executives around the world how to become better leaders using this principle. By being authentic about your values and aligning these values with those of your people, you can ignite a passionate, natural commitment toward whatever you are building. Michael Feiner, the former chief people officer of Pepsi and current member of my advisory board, calls this *the law of building a cathedral.*[7] He believes that great leaders must create meaning. They must connect their people with the idea that they are building something grand.

My cousin-in-law moved to New York from Germany to join a fascinating start-up called *Holstee*. On the surface, Holstee is simply two brothers who like to design T-shirts. But their company is driven by uncommon purpose, and they articulated their philosophy into what they call the Holstee Manifesto, available online and on posters. The manifesto caught fire. It was retweeted 100,000 times, and the company cannot keep up with the demand for posters.

THIS IS YOUR LIFE.
DO WHAT YOU LOVE, AND DO IT OFTEN.
IF YOU DON'T LIKE SOMETHING, CHANGE IT.
IF YOU DON'T LIKE YOUR JOB, QUIT.
IF YOU DON'T HAVE ENOUGH TIME, STOP WATCHING TV.
IF YOU ARE LOOKING FOR THE LOVE OF YOUR LIFE, STOP;
THEY WILL BE WAITING FOR YOU WHEN YOU
START DOING THINGS YOU LOVE.
STOP OVER ANALYZING, LIFE IS SIMPLE.
ALL EMOTIONS ARE BEAUTIFUL.
WHEN YOU EAT, APPRECIATE EVERY LAST BITE.
OPEN YOUR MIND, ARMS, AND HEART TO NEW THINGS
AND PEOPLE, WE ARE UNITED IN OUR DIFFERENCES.
ASK THE NEXT PERSON YOU SEE WHAT THEIR PASSION IS,
AND SHARE YOUR INSPIRING DREAM WITH THEM.
TRAVEL OFTEN; GETTING LOST WILL HELP YOU FIND YOURSELF.
SOME OPPORTUNITIES ONLY COME ONCE, SEIZE THEM.
LIFE IS ABOUT THE PEOPLE YOU MEET, AND
THE THINGS YOU CREATE WITH THEM
SO GO OUT AND START CREATING.
LIFE IS SHORT.
LIVE YOUR DREAM AND SHARE YOUR PASSION.

Source: "The Holstee Manifesto." ©2009 Written by Dave, Mike & Fabian. Design by Rachael. www.Holstee.com/Manifesto

That is the power of being good. Your customers care as much about who you are as a company as they do about the efficacy of your product, and because they do, they want you and your product to succeed.

■ ■ ■

If you have ever dreamed of transforming an industry and helping others in the process, you want to learn from Best Doctors, a global provider of an innovative employee health benefit that improves the quality and cost of health care. It has rapidly emerged as a $100 million business with the potential to grow 10 times larger. This company gives solid proof, if anyone still needs convincing, that it is possible to make a profit by doing good.

I got a chance to meet with Best Doctors' president, Evan Falchuk, in his Boston offices, and I learned a bit of his personal story.

Falchuk graduated from Penn Law School but quickly grew restless in the legal profession. He talked with his father, a physician who had founded Best Doctors, about finding meaning and purpose, and his father said, "Come here for a little while." Falchuk quickly engaged with the company's mission—to make sure everyone gets the right medical care—and the impact the service has on individuals.

Evan experienced firsthand the stories of patients that Best Doctors helped. One was of a woman who had gone blind and was told she had a brain tumor. Because her employer was a Best Doctors client, she could ask Best Doctors for a second opinion. Best Doctors assembled her medical records and found she could have a rare version of sarcoidosis, the collection of fatty tissue. The diagnosis saved the patient from undergoing brain surgery for a nonexistent tumor, her sarcoidosis was treated, and today she can see.

A Tool for Solving Social Problems

We have seen how a for-profit company realizes a strategic benefit from adopting a social purpose. But it makes equal sense for a social cause to adopt a for-profit model.

Michael Milken—unfortunately known to many as the king of junk bonds—has unleashed a stream of innovations to tackle global social problems through a network of organizations, including FasterCures/The Center for Accelerating Medical Solutions, the Melanoma Research Alliance, the Milken Family Foundation, the Prostate Cancer Foundation, the Milken Institute, the Milken Scholars Program, the Epilepsy Research Awards program, Mike's Math Club, Knowledge Universe Education, and Knowledge Learning Corporation. The breadth of his work makes it difficult to summarize the effect he has had. But Larry King encapsulated Milken's impact on cancer, one of Milken's key themes, saying, "When they cure this disease [cancer] they'll have to call it the *Milken cure.*"[8]

Here's Milken himself on the strategic benefit of pursuing social and profit goals simultaneously:

> *Even before going to Wharton and then joining a Wall Street firm in 1969, I'd developed a formula that says prosperity in any society depends on the leveraging effect of financial technology on the sum of human capital, social capital and real assets. Real assets are typical balance sheet items: cash, receivables, land, buildings, etc. Social capital includes educational, cultural, religious and medical institutions and such intangibles as the rule of law and enforceable property rights. Human capital—the largest, most important asset—is the ability and productivity of people.*[9]

We are seeing a rapid emergence of innovative thinkers like Milken using for-profit principles to tackle social problems.

When Gyanesh Pandey and Ratnesh Yadav, friends from childhood, decided to take on the challenge of bringing electricity to rural towns in India, they had to overcome two types of challenges. First was the technical challenge, which they solved by developing a small generator that can run on discarded rice husks. Burning the rice husks from one village created enough energy to power the entire village for 10 hours. But that still left the broader challenge of spreading these mini–power plants throughout rural India.

The two friends thought about forming a nonprofit, but in the end, they realized that this path would not lead them as far as they could go if they could find a way to make their mission profitable. With some creative strategizing, they designed a business model that works for everyone: villagers get light, and investors get a return on their investment. They have won the financial support of numerous venture capitalists for their company, Husk Power Systems, and are now bringing light to hundreds of villages.

Another example is Better Place, an Israeli company that creates systems and infrastructure that support the use of electric cars. The company's founder, Shai Agassi, is pursuing a social mission—to free the world from dependency on oil—with a profitable solution: creating a smart grid of battery-charging terminals and battery-switch stations that make it easier for a consumer to switch on an electric car battery than fill up a gas tank.

Soon after its founding, Better Place raised $200 million in funding, making it the fifth largest start-up in history. It now has presence in China, Japan, Australia, the United States, Canada, France, and Denmark.

Another client that I work with has built itself into one of the largest distributors of bulk foods in the United States. It helps small to mid-sized grocery chains manage their bulk foods aisles and, in exchange, provides the inventory for a profit. Although the company's corporate focus is growth and customer service, underpinning its purpose is a much bigger mission. Its official goal, publicized only internally, is to give away $10 million per year to charity. The company does not want me to share its name because it wishes to donate anonymously.

These ventures exemplify how companies that embrace this being good concept think. They do not just slap on go green marketing campaigns as a new corporate branding tool. They sometimes even avoid public recognition of the good they're doing. They do this because they trust that doing good will come back to benefit them in some way, even if they cannot right now see or predict the chain of events that will benefit them. They adopt being good as a strategy for a complex world. That is the principle of Karma.

■ ■ ■

Few people know Valley Forge Fabrics by name, but if you've ever stayed in a hotel or sat in a hotel lobby, then you have probably experienced the company's products. This once-small mom-and-pop business now sells more decorative upholstery fabrics to the hospitality industry than any other company in the world.

Valley Forge Fabrics was founded by a husband-and-wife team who had a simple idea: to sell high-quality fabrics to hotels. Over the past three decades, the company has emerged as the largest player in its niche.

To be sure, its success is due in part to an innovative sourcing strategy—just as Dell jumped over retailers, Valley Forge jumps over fabric dealers to buy fabrics directly from small factories in Asia. But the company also has a strong focus on sustainability, and I'm convinced it's a key reason for their success. It's not just lip service—it is a directive from upper management and a mission of the entire company.

Valley Forge Fabrics has made an effort to recycle everything it can. It is the first to produce a fabric made entirely of postconsumer waste (e.g., used paper and cotton). It encourages recycling in many other ways, both large and small. There's a place for employees to bring in their old Croc shoes for recycling, and Monday is the day for bringing in your old wine corks.

The company has also developed a program to reuse hospitality linens. Most of the time, when a hotel is done with its sheets, it just throws them away. That's hundreds of millions of pounds of lightly frayed sheets heading to landfills. Valley Forge Fabrics picks up old linens (after they have been washed one last time) and then delivers them to homeless shelters or rehabilitation centers within 200 miles of that particular hotel.

Beyond recycling, Valley Forge Fabrics has spent the past two years developing a new line of sheets made with a renewable resource. After a couple of less-than-satisfactory tries with cotton and bamboo, they found that eucalyptus pulp can be turned into a fiber by using only one organic solvent. So the company began working with Lenzing, an Austrian company that uses eucalyptus to make a clothing fabric called *Tencel*, and together they produced Tencel Plus, the first eucalyptus-based fabric strong enough to withstand the industrial washers hotels use and soft enough to satisfy the most luxurious hotels.

By passionately focusing a social mission, Valley Forge Fabrics spurs creativity and produces innovations that competitors have difficulty keeping up with.

Conclusion

Companies that are winning today talk more about doing good than their less successful competitors—and it's not just talk. They are at the front of a fundamental shift from the old greed is good mentality, which sets corporations up as slaves to shareholders, to a new view that advises companies to pursue strategies that are good to a broader set of stakeholders—employees, the community, the environment, and so on. My research shows, statistically, that companies that embrace this new paradigm enjoy a more complete competitive advantage.

CHAPTER 7

Create Something Out of Nothing

What we call reality is an agreement that people have arrived at to make life more livable.

—Louise Nevelson[1]

Traditional Playbook	New Playbook
Play with the pieces on the board, with the players in the game.	Create and remove pieces and players as needed.

The innovations that have had the greatest impact on our world are invisible. We cannot touch, feel, or smell them, but nonetheless they exert a transformative force. Take, for example, humankind's original innovation: the scratch plow. Some 5,000 years ago a farmer picked up a three-pronged stick that gave him an idea. He stuck one prong into the ground, tied the other prong to an ox, and used the third prong to guide a line that he dug through the dirt and planted seeds. At the end of the season, for the first time ever, he had more food than he needed. Farming was born. Over time this invention transformed most of humankind from hunter-gatherers into farmers. All because one man picked up a stick and thought not "firewood" but "plow."

Take a look at that first stick, though. Physically, it looked like any other three-pronged stick. It would have made great firewood. What triggered the innovation, which led to an agrarian society, was the *concept* of a plow, not the physical artifact.

If this way of thinking—a concept rather than a tangible item, which I think holds the key to innovation—seems too abstract, let's take a look at an invention a little closer to home. This one began in China around 3000 BC, when merchants had the idea of mingling their goods and distributing them across many different boats, rather than each merchant's loading all his goods onto one boat. This way, if a boat sank, the loss to any one merchant would be minimal. In other words, merchants bound together to spread out the risk. Insurance was born.

About 2,400 years later, ancient Greeks, and later the Romans, formed benevolent societies. If a member of such a society died, the society would pay for that member's funeral costs and take care of the family left behind. Death insurance was born. The idea gained much greater popularity in the 1700s, when it sold under the more palatable name life insurance.

Without such invisible inventions, civilization would surely not exist. We would not have evolved from small bands of hunter-gatherers into communities of farmers and then into the highly interdependent, specialized societies we live in today.

In each case the pattern is clear. Someone experiences some pain (e.g., the person starves through a bad hunting season, loses a ship). Looking to avoid or improve this situation in the future, the person invents something invisible—a new concept, a new social construction, such as farming or insurance. This new concept brings people together to make the world more predictable. Society evolves.

> Some categories really are social constructions: they exist only because people tacitly agree to act as if they exist. Examples include money, tenure, citizenship, decorations for bravery, and the presidency of the United States.
>
> —*Steven Pinker,* The Blank Slate[2]

Today, we see great companies continuing the tradition of "creating something out of nothing." Apple creates the iPod, which it claims is not an MP3 player but an entirely new concept, and then the iPad, positioned as a brand new class of device, not just another tablet computer. In a moment we'll take a look at how Aflac invented a concept—and I don't mean the duck—which propelled the small family-owned insurer into a global giant.

■ ■ ■

The game of business is played with a rule that does not actually exist. The players follow this rule because it exists in most of the games they are already familiar with. The rule is this: *you cannot add a new piece to the board.*

Think about it. In chess you cannot add a new queen. You cannot put an additional player on the field in a football game. I play a board game with my kids in which the goal is get rid of all your penguins by balancing them on an iceberg, and although I sometimes wish I could add a few more penguins to my kids' piles, the rules clearly say I cannot. I checked.

The only ones who do not play by this rule are today's outthinkers. Because they don't, they are able to surprise their opponents. By creating things out of nothing—a new category, for example—outthinkers catch their competitors off guard. Apple has a long tradition of doing this.

One month before Apple released the first iPad, I was conducting a strategic thinking workshop for a group of technology executives. We were exploring the pending release, assessing its potential and its strategic implications. Shockingly, at least in hindsight, this group of smart, tech-savvy executives all arrived at the same conclusion: the iPad would have limited success, and its ripple on the strategic dynamics of its industry would be barely felt.

They reached this conclusion because they were thinking about the pieces on the board, ignoring how things could change if new pieces were added—in this case, a new category. We now know that this logic was flawed. The experts characterized the iPad as a tablet, but customers did not. To them it was something entirely new. Among the experts caught by surprise was Michael Dell, who said, "I didn't completely see that coming."[3]

The iPad quickly accelerated onto one of the fastest growth curves of new consumer technologies, selling more out of the gates than the Nintendo DS, Sony PSP, iPhone, and other breakthrough devices. Its sales spilled out far beyond the traditionally defined tablet market, deflated the once-fast-growing netbook category practically overnight, and quickly became Apple's third largest source of revenue, after the iPod and the Mac.

Apple is by no means the only company adept at creating something out of nothing. We can trace the success of many breakthrough companies to the same strategy.

- Gatorade beat out Coca-Cola and Pepsi by creating the sports drink category.
- When Fredric Rosen decided to raise service fees and split them with concert venues, rather than charging venues as his competitor Ticketron did, he created an entirely new business model and grew Ticketmaster into a $2.5 billion business before leaving in 1998.
- When Nintendo's deal to license the Popeye character fell through, they needed a way to salvage the countless hours its video game developers had invested, so they created their own character—a chubby plumber named Mario—and brought a new generation of players into the video game market.
- Instead of selling real goods—as nearly every other company on the planet does—an innovative online video game company called *Zynga* generates millions of dollars in donations by selling virtual goods to its players.[4]
- De Beers created the tradition of giving diamond engagement rings and thereby generated billions of dollars in diamond sales.
- Candy manufacturers in Japan and South Korea created White Day, a made-up holiday that occurs 30 days after Valentine's Day. On White Day, men must reciprocate the multiple Valentine gifts they received from the women in their lives: wives, daughters, mothers, and coworkers. That's a lot of candy.

So, although there are a number of examples of companies creating something out of nothing, what has changed today is that it has become a requisite capability, versus the once-in-a-generation event it was historically. My research shows that today's outthinkers embrace this strategy far more readily than their competitors—and they generate superior growth and profitability as a result.

Anatomy of the Strategy

Some interesting scientific findings help us dissect how this strategy unfolds and why it is so successful.

1. Your competitors stop thinking. This pressure to stop thinking has evolutionary roots, as Paul Glimcher, of NYU's Center for Neural Science, explains, "Evolution, we have to believe, provided a very strong pressure for animals to do the smart thing, that is to find a final common path, a common valuation, and make decisions based on it."[5] This final common path is formalized by the market, so it becomes much easier to prove the viability of product that fits an existing category than one that creates a new category. Try pitching an idea to a skeptical boss without being able to say, "The market for tablet PCs is projected to grow *x* percent over the next five years."
2. Someone adopts an inconsistent frame of the world. Jeff Bezos, chief executive officer (CEO) of Amazon, for example was asked at a conference to describe what business his company was in and he characterized Amazon not as a retailer but as a protector of its customers' personal data.
3. That person creates a new category by introducing a product or service that does not fit the existing category. The competitor's mirror neurons, which we discussed in Chapter 6, fail to fire because they do not recognize the new category. The competitors have never experienced a sports drink or an iPad before, so they cannot imagine the product succeeding. As a result, they dismiss the product's potential.
4. The competition eventually wakes up. Just as scientific anomalies in Kuhn's world attract the attention of the scientific community, the outthinker's anomaly attracts the attention of competitors. But if the

outthinker plans his or her strategy well, the competition takes too long to reorient itself from the old category and responds too slowly to stop the innovator.

Construct Your Destination

On an overnight flight home from Ecuador, I was dead tired but couldn't fall asleep. My mind was buzzing. I had just conducted a seminar for a group of some 70 CEOs who collectively represented about 30 percent of Ecuador's gross domestic product (GDP). *Harvard Business Review* had gathered them together to network and learn, and they asked me to facilitate the session. These leaders assembled in a banquet room, brainstorming creative strategies for solving a critical challenge: How can we turn Quito, Ecuador's capital, into a major tourist destination?

What kept me awake on that long flight was the realization that the best strategies for enhancing tourism are also used skillfully by some of the world's best-known products. The core idea is the same: create something out of nothing. The world is opening in ways unimagined. Tourists are pouring into China, India, and Dubai, places that 10 years ago were visited by only the most daring. And yet, the number-one tourist country continues to be France. It attracts 70 to 80 million visitors per year, almost 50 percent more than the two countries tied for second place. China's Great Wall, Australia's Great Barrier Reef, and India's 5,000 years of history cannot compete with France.

But what is France? A place, or an idea? Why do more tourists visit Paris than any other city in the world? Ask a few who have been there, and you will get a montage of responses—cafés, baguettes, croissants, the Eiffel Tower, the Arc de Triomphe, wine, ornate architecture, windy streets, and so on—that together create what the world knows to be Paris. Yet this Paris is dramatically different from the one Parisians live in. Few of the things *Paris* conjures up for tourists are part of a Parisian's everyday life.

Destinations that hold great brand value have been smart in how they shaped their mental destination: *Costa Rica* means parrots, jungles, and surfing; *Jamaica* means Bob Marley and beaches; *Disney* means Mickey Mouse, family, and castles; *Las Vegas* means crazy things happening in hotel rooms; *New Orleans* means jazz, Bourbon Street, and great food—the list goes on.

The critical insight here is that your customers are probably less attracted by what your product actually is than by the image they have constructed in their minds. Managing the symbols and associations your customers have with your product or service is an art. Be strategic about it, and you can wire a web in their brains that captures their interest and gives them warm feelings that makes them want more.

Create an Occasion

At 11 PM in a bar, after a few drinks with a group of friends (assuming you are of the right age range), someone eventually and naturally comes up with an idea: "Let's get a round of tequila shots!" Who put this idea in your head? Tequila makers, of course. They have for years been strategically building and reinforcing the *tequila occasion.*

This ability to create an occasion for your product is more than a marketing tactic. For innovative products it becomes a critical skill. Too many great inventions have failed simply because their inventors were unable to imbed an occasion in the minds of users.

Procter & Gamble (P&G), for example, nearly pulled the plug on one of its most successful new product launches, Febreze, because no one was buying. But giving it one more shot, they changed the imagery in their advertising from women unpacking sweaters pulled down from the attic to women making beds with fresh-smelling sheets.

By linking your product or service to your customers' environments, you can trigger the proper response. The idea of pulling out sweaters at the end of the summer happens too rarely (just once per year) to offer a useful product hook. So P&G had to give it a new identity and a repeating image—make bed, spray Febreze; make bed, spray Febreze; make bed, spray Febreze. They created the Febreze occasion.

"If It Quacks Like a Duck . . . "

Before 1992, even loyal customers struggled to recall the name of the American Family Life Assurance Company. But today, customers and noncustomers alike, indeed anyone in the United States or Japan who watches television, cannot take a summer stroll past a park pond without thinking, or maybe even saying to themselves, "Aflac."

How did a small, family-owned, run-of-the-mill insurance company from Georgia evolve into a $20 billion icon with a brand as infectious as Ronald McDonald or Mickey Mouse? I recently had the chance to sit down with Daniel P. Amos, Aflac's CEO, and my conclusion is that although the Aflac duck may appear to be the star of the company's story, it really plays only a supporting role. At the heart of Aflac's success is the strategy of creating something out of nothing.

It is perhaps inaccurate to call Aflac an American company. Sure, it was founded by three brothers from Georgia post–World War II. And yes, it remains family run, and CEO Amos still lives in a small Georgia town and speaks with a cultured southern drawl. However, the company generates more than 70 percent of its revenues from, and attributes more than 80 percent of its assets to, its Japanese operations.

This success in Japan can be traced to an insight derived from simple mathematics. By the early 1970s the Japanese were living longer, and at the same time, the number of cancer deaths was growing dramatically. "The Japanese were scared that there was an epidemic of cancer taking place, back in 1974 when we were licensed [in Japan to sell cancer insurance]," Amos explained. "The fact is there wasn't an epidemic. What was going on was the life expectancy of the Japanese had gone from 58 or 59, and it had jumped to 84. People were then just living long enough to get cancer."

This built a demand for a new type of insurance, and Aflac met that demand. "We became the first company to be licensed after the war," Amos said. "At that time, they had two basic insurance markets—they had the non-life and the life. The life was called *sector one*. We created what we call the third sector . . . a cancer insurance policy . . . It paid X amount if you died for any reason, but if you died of cancer, it paid ten times that amount."[6]

For this new type of insurance, Aflac convinced the Japanese government to give it a temporary monopoly. For seven years, Aflac would be the only insurance company that could sell cancer insurance in Japan.

That seven-year cushion gave Aflac enough of an advantage that, even decades after the monopoly protection ended, the company held on to nearly the entire market. By 1990, Aflac commanded a 90 percent market share of cancer insurance. In 1992, when the company officially changed its name from American Family Life Assurance Company to Aflac, its market share was even stronger at 94 percent.

Conclusion

The strategy of creating something out of nothing has been a trusted move of outthinkers for millennia. It works because it freezes the competition, forcing them into inaction as they go through the mental reprogramming needed to reconceptualize their model of the world. This was just as true 5,000 years ago, when China invented the concept of life insurance, as it was 40 years ago, when Aflac invented the concept of cancer insurance. What has changed is the frequency with which new things are being created.

Because much of what we buy today are social constructions rather than tangible goods and because even our purchase decisions around tangible goods are driven by softer cognitive forces such as nostalgia, springtime, and fresh air, the ability to create something out of nothing is becoming a necessary skill. Winning companies are using this tactic at an accelerating pace. Learn to recognize when your competitors are using it against you, or you risk falling behind. Better yet, learn to do it yourself.

PART 3

The Five Habits of Outthinkers

At the heart of outthinking the competition sits one fundamental question: How do some people see and seize strategic options that others overlook? I've studied some of history's most creative strategists, from Sun Tzu to Napoleon Bonaparte to Mohandas Gandhi, and had the opportunity to get into the minds of some of their modern peers—like the social and business leaders I mention in this book. I've had the opportunity to coach some amazingly creative leaders and train 5,000 people so far on the topic of strategic creativity. If we mash all of these experiences together, contrasting the thought processes of outthinkers with the rest of us, we see five key habits that lead outthinkers toward seeing and realizing unorthodox solutions:

1. Mental time travel
2. Attack of the interconnected system
3. Frame-shifting
4. Disruptive mind-set
5. Perception shaping

How some people naturally arrive at these habits, I am not sure. But I do know they can be learned. If we strengthen our muscles in these five areas, we begin to see and seize solutions that others overlook. If we can develop these habits in our team and across our company, we start to unlock the inert creative potential of our organizations. We free people to find pathways through challenges that we once thought were unworkable. We can help make the impossible possible every day.

CHAPTER 8

Mental Time Travel

Most people are not really free. They are confined by the niche in the world that they carve out for themselves. They limit themselves to fewer possibilities by the narrowness of their vision.

—V. S. Naipaul, Nobel laureate, literature 2001[1]

Imagination rules the world.

—Napoleon Bonaparte[2]

Vermont was a refreshing respite from the Miami heat. I was there to deliver a talk and arrived early enough the day before to stroll around the small college town. Whether by luck or destiny, it just so happened that a famous Buddhist monk was speaking that same evening, so I sat in on his lecture. Of the insights he sprinkled throughout the talk, the one that stuck most was his observation that Buddhist monks expend intense effort building control over their thoughts because people need such control to deeply think through big problems.

Ask people who have had a major impact on their industry or some part of the world what they were thinking in the early days when they built the belief in their cause, and they are likely to take you along in a mental time machine. At the start, they were able to fast-forward in time, imagining a desired future. When most people's minds would wander, these outthinkers were able to hold their minds steady at that moment and paint in all the detail, exploring everything that would need to happen for their vision to be realized.

Cognitive scientists call this ability to visualize a possible future mental time travel and believe it serves as a key distinction between humans and animals. This ability to imagine a possible future and then work backward to make more informed choices is a requisite of everything we call civilization. It is because of this ability that we take the time to build tools, to plant seeds, or to store food for the winter.

In humans (and a few animals, to a minor degree), this ability is innate, but it turns out we develop it over time, through practice, some of us to a higher degree than others.

When not traveling, I try to drop my two older kids off at school. As soon as we walk through the door, the three of us invariably begin an animated debate. The topic is always the same: who should be dropped off to the classroom first. My son, Lucas, who is five, wants to drop his sister off first so he can see her room; my daughter, Kaira, age three, because she wants whatever her big brother wants, naturally wants us to drop Lucas off first. I use various techniques to negotiate an agreement—some more successful than others—and I have been fascinated to note that there is one argument that sometimes works with my son but never works for my daughter.

The argument goes something like this. I kneel down to look my son in his eyes (I read in some parenting book this helps) and say, "Lucas, how about this: if we drop you off first today, then tomorrow we'll drop Kaira off first?" Lucas' eyes glaze over, he stares out into space, and you can see he is imagining tomorrow, dropping off his sister first. He is traveling mentally into the future. He then travels back to the present, and you see his eyes come alive again. And then there is a 50-50 chance that he will agree. It doesn't always work, but at least it improves my odds.

Now when I offer this argument to my daughter, she invariably, instantaneously, says "no." That is because children do not develop the ability of mental time travel until after the age of three. Scientists have tested this. They've given children the option of having two stickers tomorrow or one sticker today. Children younger than three almost always choose one sticker today. Those older than three may choose to wait for two stickers tomorrow.

Our ability to mentally time travel continues developing with experience and practice. But even after we reach adulthood, it is hard for most of us to push our minds out into a brand-new future. This is an important concept for business leaders. It is hard to plan for something you cannot imagine, and if you cannot imagine something entirely new, it is difficult to create something truly new. Great innovators instinctively understand this and put effort into developing their ability to think forward and visualize future states.

Alexandra Kosteniuk, the reigning women's world chess champion, began practicing chess seriously at a very young age. Even now, she trains heavily to continue building her skills to stay at the top of the game. She described to me how she thinks about future moves:

> *Many nonchess players think that you should mostly use intuition when playing chess. And, indeed, it is necessary to have a good imagination so you can collect a range of 'candidate moves.' But you still have to go through all the verification for each move, thinking of all the medium- and long-term strategy goals. Skipping this step will lead to many errors. Intuition can sometimes be 100 percent correct, but you still have to check everything with all the means you have available. Before playing a move, every chess player should always ask himself, 'What if that move is actually a big mistake?' Then you do a final check for correctness and harmony with the chosen plan.*[3]

I asked her how many moves out she thinks while she plays. "That totally depends on the position at hand," she said. "In some positions, especially in the endgame, it is vital to see many, many moves ahead, at least 20."

People say that President Barack Obama plays "3D chess"—a reference to the game Dr. Spock played on the original *Star Trek* television series. It's made up of multiple chess boards, one floating on top of the other, so that each piece can move along the horizontal plane but also up or down. People who have worked with (or against) Obama are saying that he thinks many moves out but also thinks across multiple planes.

In business you want to think across three planes. These are the same three planes that Sun Tzu advised generals to consider when planning for battle:[4]

1. *You:* Sun Tzu called this *man*. It represents what you, your team, or your organization wishes to accomplish. This is your mission and vision.
2. *The environment:* Sun Tzu called this *heaven* or the *sky*. It represents all that is outside of the control of the people in your game, the atmosphere in which you must achieve the vision you set above. It includes things like interest rates, jobless rates, capital flows, and gross domestic product (GDP) growth. If you have ever conducted a scenario planning exercise, this is the step where you consider your potential scenarios.
3. *Other players:* Sun Tzu called this *ground*. It represents, in our application, everything that is in control of the other players in your game. It encompasses the potential actions of your competitors, suppliers, distributors, regulators, and so forth. Game theory would fit here.

Outthinkers travel mentally toward a future. They imagine that future across multiple planes. They imagine what they want, what the environment will look like, and what competitors and other players will be doing. They paint in all of the details of that future image. They write it down on paper, or they hold the image firmly in their minds. With this vivid future completely defined, they are able to focus their efforts on what must be changed to convert the current state of things (the current picture) into the desired future.

Every great achievement was a vision before it became a reality.

—*Henry Kissinger*[5]

One of my favorite stories that illustrates the power of this mental time travel ability comes from *Master of the Senate,* volume 3 of Robert Caro's splendid biography of Lyndon B. Johnson. Here Caro describes how Johnson defined in detail the end state he desired to achieve:[6]

Defeating the [Bricker] amendment and thereby preserving the power of the presidency—his first objective—could not be accomplished even if he united his party's liberal and moderate senators against it; there simply were not enough of them. He would have to turn conservative senators against it too, conservatives who were at the moment wholeheartedly for it—and not just Democratic conservatives but at least a few member[s] of the Republican Old Guard.

Caro goes on to describe a tangle of conditions that Johnson also had to achieve, including creating a public narrative of the Republican Old Guard fighting the president (even though they would actually be voting with the president's wishes) while the Democrats were to be seen as saving the president.

The picture that Johnson created was intricate and detailed, but it was also clear. By holding this clear picture in his mind, something few would have the mental control for, Johnson would find a brilliant winning move that brought all the elements of his picture into place.

The ability to hold your mind over the problem is key to problem solving. Or, as Albert Einstein once said, "It's not that I'm so smart, it's just that I stay with problems longer."[7]

■ ■ ■

Elon Musk attended Wharton Business School around the same time I did, and then went on to an incredible career. He bought PayPal in its infancy and led the company to become the dominant player in online payments. When eBay bought PayPal, the transaction made Musk and his partners wealthy.

Musk then went on to lead two breakthrough companies. One is called *SpaceX*, one of the first private space launch companies. In 2008 I asked him why he thought his SpaceX company would succeed. His response was that he thought that "a future in which private companies shoot satellites into space instead of just the government was a more exciting future."

Sure, to realize his vision, multiple issues would need to be resolved, including building up sufficient scale before investment ran out, as well as the privatization of the U.S. government space program (and others around the world) and new global laws and norms. Some of these challenges were in Musk's control. Others were mostly in the control of others (such as the U.S. government deciding to close the NASA Space Shuttle program). These big challenges would scare most people away from the effort. But to outthinkers they are simply parts of the painting, colors, and lines that must be filled in to complete the masterpiece.

Several pieces have already begun to come together. The U.S. space program, NASA, completed its final shuttle mission on July 21, 2011, and SpaceX successfully launched its first rocket on December 8, 2010. The company is well positioned to be anointed as one of probably three private companies the United States will contract with to continue the country's space program.

Musk is applying the same thinking process to his other breakthrough company: Tesla Motors, the first U.S. automobile company to issue an IPO since Ford Motor Company in 1956. He took the reins of Tesla Motors in October 2008 and produced an electric sports car. The next four and a half years he invested approximately $70 million of his own money and helped raise another $70 million from entrepreneurs and venture capital firms.

When Musk took over as chief executive officer (CEO), the company had overcome many of the technical challenges associated with producing an electric sports car but still faced a number of business hurdles. It operated far below the scale required to make the business profitable, for example. By January 2009, Tesla had delivered just 147 cars.[8] Operating costs exceeded revenue, and it was unclear where funding would come from to fuel the company's effort to reach profitability.

Musk maintained the company's focus on a big, long-term mission: "to help expedite the move from a mine-and-burn hydrocarbon economy towards a solar electric economy."[9] With a clear focus, it becomes easy to identify what a company must untangle to realize its vision.

Musk successfully navigated Tesla through its key challenges. In May 2009, Tesla sold 10 percent of its stock to Daimler for a reported $50 million, securing both needed capital and a powerful strategic partner.[10] (Be sure to read about the first meeting with Daimler in Chapter 12.) The next month, Tesla was approved to receive nearly $500 million in interest-bearing loans from the U.S. Department of Energy as part of a program to promote advanced vehicle technology. Two months after that, Tesla reported its first profitable month. Just one month later, in September 2009, the company announced it had raised another $82.5 million. In June 2010, Toyota agreed to buy $50 million of the company's soon-to-be publicly traded stock. In July, Tesla issued an IPO, raising $226 million. Its stock rose 41 percent on its first day of trading.[11]

Conclusion

The ability to travel mentally forward in time is a key distinguisher between humans and animals. We all begin developing this ability around the age of three. Some of us continue developing this for many years, and a few of us become quite advanced. Outthinkers, I believe, have a heightened ability. As a result, they advance where others hold back, they see things as possible that others cannot fathom, and they are able to see "reasons something won't work" as simply "issues that remain to be resolved."

CHAPTER 9

Attacking the Interconnected System

To manage a system effectively, you might focus on the interactions of the parts rather than their behavior taken separately.

—Russell Ackoff[1]

In war, events of importance are the result of trivial causes.

—Julius Caesar[2]

When Scipio Africanus took on the seemingly impossible task of defeating Hannibal in 205 BC, he resisted the direct assault that other Roman military leaders had tried before him. Instead, as we saw in Chapter 1, he did the exact opposite and turned the other direction, toward Carthage. Capturing that city meant he cut Hannibal off from its supply lines. The once indomitable enemy was now severely weakened, and the Romans were finally able to vanquish him.

The critical lesson from this story is not counterintuitive thinking—although that is important—but the fact that Scipio Africanus took in a bigger picture, looking not just at the players but at their interdependencies. By studying the entire interconnected system, he found a masterstroke that would weaken his enemy with minimal effort.

In the West we might call this systems thinking. The Taoists began speaking of this ability five millennia ago, advocating the appreciation of the interconnectedness of all things. This is how outthinkers think. While their competitors focus on the parts of the system (e.g., Hannibal), they look also at the invisible interconnections (e.g., the flow of supplies). To borrow a Taoist analogy, while others see the spokes of a wheel, outthinkers see the empty center that makes the wheel move. Following interconnections and dependencies of the system, outthinkers often discover new points of leverage to attack; thus they can change the system more quickly and more easily. This is like a doctor who seeks to diagnose and address the causes of a sickness rather than just seeking to make symptoms go away.

Most of us tend to focus on the subject of the system and not so much on its context. For example, when we talk about the evolution of the automobile, we tend to cite the car itself—the internal technology and their manufacturing innovations—but we ignore advances in road construction that make the modern automobile possible. This came to me with a thud when I was visiting my mother in Malawi, a small country in eastern Africa. After two hours, as we were approaching our destination, we had to turn off the regular paved road onto a dirt one. The red earth had developed ruts from cars constantly driving on it and the regularity of their pattern created a vibration that made it impossible to drive faster than 30 miles per hour. A nice modern car stymied by an old road.

When two Canadian engineers at Research in Motion (RIM) took on the challenge of building a mobile device for the U.S. market, they could have taken the proven route: Build a product that users will love, launch an effective marketing campaign, ramp up sales to achieve economies of scale that allow you to sell it at a competitive price, and then keep improving the product incrementally to stay ahead of competitive copycats. This is the standard model. If you execute it well, it works.

But instead, the team attacked a part of the system no one else was paying attention to. All of RIM's competitors were starting to sell mobile phones, abandoning an older device, the pager, which could deliver only text information. They were building a new network of towers that could transmit text and voice. RIM saw an opportunity. The company designed a device that used the old, abandoned text network, with plenty of excess capacity, in an innovative way to transmit two-way text messages.

Their new device was ugly and could transmit only text. End users probably would have preferred one of Motorola's cooler new cell phones. But RIM was selling to end users—specifically, corporations—and pitching the product as a device that could deliver e-mails to their employees faster and more reliably than anything else. They called it the *BlackBerry*.

The rest of the story is well known. RIM grew to dominate the corporate sector. It could have introduced a BlackBerry with voice long before it actually did, but the company held back because it understood the strategic value of the system. It was playing with a point of leverage that no one else had their hands on. Once RIM had built a strong enough base in the corporate market, it began branching out into the consumer market with devices that offered text, voice, and even Internet content.

The lesson is this: If you attack the obvious parts of the system, the only way to do better than your competition is to execute better. This is riskier and more tiring. If, instead, you step back and look at the entire system, paying attention to the invisible interconnections, you may find a way to win faster and with greater ease.

Here is another fun example of attacking the system and isolating key leverage points. If you put one small coin, such as a penny, on the track in front of every wheel of a standing train, the train will be unable to move. Overcoming those little coins is the same as having the train overcome a single column of all the coins stuck together. I do not know if this has actually been tested, but laws of physics say it is true.

■ ■ ■

Talk to successful executives about how they engineered their success, and you are likely to find they have developed a mental systems map of the key leverage points. Once they have identified the key points of leverage, they can replicate their formula. What starts out as a complex unorthodox strategy becomes a simple model that guides them day after day and keeps them focused on what's important. Take, for example, Knoa Software.

When Thad Eidman decided to jump into a start-up, he did so with both eyes open and a secret formula in mind. Before launching Knoa, a fast-growing software firm that helps companies like British Telecom and DHL get more value out of their enterprise software, Eidman had already honed his secret formula. He was previously entrepreneur-in-residence at Constellation Ventures, a New York–based, $450 million venture fund. Before that, he was the cofounder and president of iFLEET/ERS, a leading provider of technology to the transportation industry. He also spent 12 years at Dun & Bradstreet (D&B), including stints at McCormack & Dodge, D&B's software division, and A.C. Nielsen, D&B's marketing research division.

During that time, he saw that companies often invest tens of millions of dollars to install a new enterprise system (e.g., Oracle, SAP) but fail to realize their full benefits because users don't adopt the program, or if they do, they do not use it efficiently. Thad reasoned that if companies could go deeper and measure how end users actually use software applications, they could address many of those issues and get the kinds of benefits the software application promised.

The reasoning seems to be working because Eidman and his team have been growing Knoa at 100 percent year after year and they now have 130 customers. Their success is due, in part, to the simplicity of their business-building approach.

When a problem looks complex, it is because you have not yet mastered it. Masters reach simplicity. As Charles Mingus, the late American jazz composer and pianist, once said, "Creativity is more than just being different. Anybody can play weird—that's easy. What's hard is to be as simple as Bach. Making the simple complicated is commonplace—making the complicated simple, awesomely simple—that's creativity."[3] Eidman's experience leads him to such simplicity.

What is Eidman's "secret formula"? In our interview, he shared his theory that a successful business has four steps:

1. Get a customer.
2. Make the customer happy.

3. Get a referral.
4. Repeat.

■ ■ ■

Over the past 10 years, my colleagues and I have interviewed several hundred chief executive officers (CEOs) and entrepreneurs to understand how they do it. When we spoke to Phil Fernandez, we realized we had hit the gold mine.

Fernandez is an entrepreneur who has already taken two companies public. Now he is applying his process again, as the CEO of Marketo, a revenue performance management company that in just a few years grew to 1,000 customers in 30 countries with a 315 percent year-over-year revenue growth rate. My colleague Nadia Laurinci and I got a chance to learn firsthand how Fernandez does it. Here is his recipe:

1. *Set out to change the world.* Identify a business opportunity where you can make a dramatic impact. Tesla Motors, whose leaders we met in Chapter 8, is pursuing a grand mission: "to increase the number and variety of electric cars available to mainstream consumers."
2. *Design a product that passes three tests.* Make sure the product you want to build is (a) valuable for the customer, (b) well-defined, and (c) unique relative to the competition. Every breakthrough product or service we could think of—Skype, the iPad, the Flip video recorder—passed these tests.
3. *Kill the plum tree.* The Chinese have a saying that you must sometimes let the plum tree wither to make room for the peach. Similarly, you will need to say "no" to business opportunities that might lure you away from your focus.
4. *Build with velocity.* Build a large and sticky customer base quickly. A company's value is often built on a story of velocity. When investors like technology guru Komisar said of a new IPO, "You can't hide the fact that this thing is slowing down. There was a year of hypergrowth, and then it rolled over,"[4] that company had to drop its offer

price from $100 to $85. Luckily the company, Google, accelerated again and made up the loss.

5. *Manage customer acquisition cost.* Figure out how you can acquire new customers at half the cost of your competitors. One of our favorite outthinkers, Vistaprint (you met this company in Chapter 1), spends next to nothing on traditional marketing. Instead, it gives away free business cards, which carry little marginal costs.

Conclusion

Outthinkers think in terms of a system, whereas their competitors focus on just the obvious nodes in the system. This lets outthinkers identify points of leverage others overlook. Regardless of how far you feel comfortable taking this—from building a simple map to defining your key priorities this week all the way to embracing the Taoist view that everything is connected—it is worth taking a pause before you begin problem solving. Study the overall system. Figure out what depends on what, then build out the web until you see clearly the fronts of your battle and the levers you must apply pressure to in order to realize your vision.

CHAPTER 10

Frame Shifting

I never came upon any of my discoveries through the process of rational thinking.

—Albert Einstein[1]

My kids were waiting in the garage, all bundled up on a cold morning, bags in hand, ready for school. I was scurrying around the living room looking for the car keys. I had searched everywhere I thought they might be but still no keys, so I got on my knees. I wasn't praying; I just didn't know what else to do, and there, behind a piece of furniture, were the keys. One of my children must have hidden them, playing a joke on Dad. Probably.

We got to school on time that morning. But we might not have if I hadn't changed my perspective. Sometimes just shifting your point of view can reveal new solutions.

Indeed, research into expertise and expert performance explains how great strategists use mental frames to break cognitive barriers that prevent others from seeing new options. It is not just that experts know more about the problem—in fact they often know less—but they think differently. They restructure, reorganize, and refine their representation of knowledge so as to more efficiently apply knowledge to solve problems.

Specifically, they overcome three limits to human thinking capacity:[2]

1. *We have a limited ability to concentrate.* We cannot perceive and pay attention to all of the stimuli we are exposed to—sight, position, time/speed, distance, and spectra/color.[3] This means we must constrain what we pay attention to.[4] What distinguishes experts is that they are able to pay attention to and remain aware of the right things more often than novices. Great chess players, for example, fixate on the most relevant squares on a chessboard and therefore make fewer calculations before choosing a move. This gives them a "perceptual head start."[5]
2. *We struggle with limited working memory capacity.* Solving a problem requires three actions: (a) we perceive data or information, (b) we bring forward relevant knowledge from our long-term memory into our short-term memory, and (c) we draw inferences about what is going on in order to choose an action or to seek additional data. Since we draw inferences only from what is in our short-term memory, our ability to solve problems is limited by our capacity to hold information there. Experts seem able to hold more information in short-term memory than novices, although this is not because they actually have larger memory capacity.
3. *We struggle with limited long-term-memory access.* We have all experienced being unable to access the relevant long-term memory, such as when something is on the tip of the tongue. We are aware that we know something but cannot retrieve it from long-term memory.[6] One reason experts are able to solve problems novices cannot is that they are less often stopped by such limits. They can more effectively access relevant knowledge from their long-term memory at the right time for short-term memory to work on.

Experts are able to overcome these cognitive limits through a process of chunking. That is, they develop a high-order vocabulary to group things into chunks, or patterns. This lets them process information more rapidly and effectively, enabling them to conceive of and implement more complex strategies. While the novice is thinking about moving the knight closer to the opponent's king, the expert is thinking about applying the Lasker-Bauer combination, and therefore more often successfully outmaneuvers his opponent.[7] In business, the expert—the outthinker—may well be outmaneuvering by shifting perspective.

For the past 10 years I have been using a set of ancient Chinese military strategies, called the *36 Stratagems,* to help entrepreneurs and executives see new frames and thereby devise innovative strategies. What I've observed is that these strategic narratives, as I call them, work like those higher-order chunks that great chess players use to dominate the board. (All 36 stratagems are in Appendix B.)

Strategic narratives are sequences of strategic moves that take advantage of short-term working memory. All I have to do is name the story and the whole plot comes up in your head. For example, if I say, "Trojan horse," then this one label pulls up a pretty complex sequence of moves and countermoves. Strategic narratives direct our attention, help us hold more information (larger chunks) in working memory, and help us access long-term memory. In other words, they help us deal with all three of the core cognitive barriers that stand between novices and experts.

Chess champion Alexandra Kosteniuk is known for performing something of a media stunt. She lines up 15 chessboards and invites 15 players to sit in front of each one. They sit and look at the boards while she stands and moves from one to the next. When she has played her first move for each of the 15 games, she starts over with the first one and makes her second move. This gives each of her opponents a lot of time to think about their next move, whereas she gets only a few seconds.

She usually wins all of the matches. Somehow she is able, in just a few seconds, to look at the board and know the winning move even though her opponent, who has perhaps 20 minutes to stare and think through the pieces and combinations, cannot see that move.

I believe Kosteniuk is using her repertoire for strategic frames or narratives. When she looks at a board, she sees not the pieces but the pattern the pieces are in and she thinks, *I recognize this game. I've played this game before, and the way to win is to do . . .*

Research into expertise and expert performance has actually been able to measure this. Master chess players recognize twice as many patterns as experts when they look at a game board in play. Grandmaster chess players are able to recognize 10 times as many.

This means your ability to see strategic options that others don't see has little to do with your innate intelligence or how creative you are. It is simply a function of the number and variety of frames—or chunks or strategic narratives—you bring to the game.

Similarly, the ability of your team to see unorthodox strategic options is a function of their diversity. The more different their natural repertoires of patterns are, the more innovative their ideas are, provided you facilitate the conversation effectively.

During my strategic thinking workshop I walk participants through five to seven strategic narratives, encouraging them to shift their frame on their strategic challenge five to seven times. We've found that on average, groups generate 6 to 10 times as many options by shifting their frames on the problem. In one session, I was conducting a workshop for about 200 executives sitting in tables of 10 people. One table generated 256 possible strategies. In another workshop, 60 chief executive officers (CEOs) of fast-growing, mid-sized companies were working individually on growth ideas. One of them generated 158 possible strategies for growing the business.

The process is simple (we'll cover it step by step in Chapter 15) but incredibly powerful. The more strategies you are able to consider, the greater the probability that you will see the silver bullet, the winning move that will take your competitors by surprise.

■ ■ ■

The second benefit of using frame shifting when you design your strategies is that it leads to more disruption. Your competitors have as much difficulty shifting their frames as you do. So when you come up with a strategy based on unorthodox frames, it disrupts your competitors. If they are to respond to you, they themselves are forced to adopt an unorthodox frame to understand what you are doing. That slows them down while you forge ahead.

I asked Dick Hayne, CEO of Urban Outfitters, one of the fastest-growing, most profitable clothing retailers in the United States why his company has been so successful. "Because we knew nothing about the business when we started," he said.[8] In other words, he and his business partner got into the retailing business using a set of frames that were foreign to retailers. As a result, they made a lot of strategic choices that made sense from their frame but that seemed impossible from the traditional perspective. For example, they chose to:

- Sell exclusively to college students while competitors sell to a broader consumer base.
- Staff stores with "sensory merchandisers" rather than analytical managers. They hire managers out of art programs rather than business schools and choose them based on their aesthetic skills rather than proven management skills.
- Decentralize store operational decisions so that every store has a different look.
- Sell used clothing along with new merchandise.
- Remove a layer of management, which reduces the level of monitoring and oversight the company can impose on stores.
- Separate merchandizing from designing so that Urban's designers—even those who are designing clothing for the company's own labels—cannot be sure that stores will carry their designs.

■ ■ ■

When the U.S. Air Force asked their best fighter pilot, John Boyd, to analyze how he trained pilots to outmaneuver even better-armed enemies, he took the task seriously. He analyzed not just his dogfights, but many of history's greatest battles, seeking to understand what great generals did to win. After years of analysis and refinement, he came up with a powerfully simple answer, one that underscores the power of being able to shift your perspective more often and more quickly than your competitors'.

His theory is that all intelligent organizations, and even organisms, win by passing more efficiently through four stages of interactions with their environments:

- *Observation.* Collecting data from multiple sources (e.g., the senses for organisms, business systems for corporations, spies for the CIA).

- *Orientation.* Analyzing and synthesizing the data to form a mental model.
- *Decision.* Deciding to take a specific set of actions based on your mental model.
- *Action.* Physically making or executing your decisions.

You have surely heard the debates about which step is most important. Many say great companies win through execution (action) while others say the key is strategy (decision). Amazon offers 1,000 books about strategy and 6,000 about execution, and if you read them, you'd think you'd have covered your bases.

But Boyd would likely agree with a newcomer on the block who says that if you cannot observe and orient well, if you can't find the unconventional strategy that disrupts your competitors, all of your execution or strategy crafting skill is useless.

Conclusion

Great strategists—outthinkers—shift frames. They attack the problem with a greater number and diversity of viewpoints. This creates two advantages: First, they see more options than others see, which makes them more likely to find the silver bullet. Second, the resulting strategy, if it is rooted in a different frame, will be more disruptive because competitors will be slow to respond. They will resist shifting their frame, giving the outthinkers a very nice head start.

CHAPTER 11

A Disruptive Mind-Set

Striking in all places and at all times, and striking by surprise are varieties of waging war with infantry.

—*The Arthashastra*[1]

Never interrupt your enemy when he is making a mistake.

—Napoleon Bonaparte[2]

In the middle of their presentation, the boss interrupted.

"What makes you think [insert archenemy's name here] can't do this just as well as us? Or better?!"

For a moment I was afraid they would freeze. I had been working with them for about six weeks, coaching them through developing a business case for an unorthodox business strategy. If their idea worked, I felt it could create ripples throughout the market: it was something that competitors, even smart and well-funded ones, would not copy.

The team was one of about 20 I was coaching. Until that time, most of our discussions centered around customers and execution. They had nailed their analyses, which showed customers would value the idea, and the company had the technical know-how to make it happen. But today, when they finally got the chance to present their ideas to senior management, the conversation shifted quickly to the competition. How long would it take others to copy it? The higher up an organization you go, I have found, the more you hear leaders thinking about the competition.

Luckily, the team was ready with answers, and the boss was satisfied. The idea was launched three months later and turned into a meaningful differentiator for the company.

Outthinkers recognize that although having a product customers love and having the ability to deliver are critical, these alone create no more than a flash of success if the idea is one the competition can easily steal from you. They may be creative as heck, but creative is not sufficient by itself. Truly effective strategies must be disruptive, meaning that they are creative *and* difficult for competitors to copy.

Just as entropy always increases and water seeks the lowest point, great ideas struggle against a natural, continuous pull of commoditization. As Bruce Greenwald, the Columbia professor known as the *guru of value investment gurus*, says, "In the long-run, everything becomes a toaster."[3] The goal is to innovate faster than your competition. That means either innovating faster, slowing down your competition, or both. Here we will cover some practical methods for doing each.

Innovate Faster

In 2008, when I moved from Miami to New York, my friend Sabrina Herrera's company went public. I had always admired Genomma Lab, an innovative Mexican pharmaceutical company, and even wrote about it in a 2004 article in the *Harvard Business Review*. When the company issued its IPO, I felt that the company, and Sabrina, had made it.

The IPO is where success stories often end, unfortunately. But for outthinkers, an IPO is like graduating from high school. It means you have come a long way but that your adventure is just beginning.

On a recent trip to Mexico, I got a chance to experience this post-IPO journey. I was in town to deliver a seminar for some 600 people, and Sabrina attended with about 10 people from her team. After the seminar Sabrina invited me to visit their brand-new 70,000-square-foot headquarters, and I got a chance to see what very few witness: the inner workings of a competitive machine.

Genomma Lab now generates more than $500 million in revenue. They've opened the second-largest pharmaceutical distribution center in Latin America. Their chief executive officer (CEO), Rodrigo Herrera, Sabrina's brother, was named the Mexican entrepreneur of the year by Ernst & Young. Genomma Lab has become the number-one pharmaceutical over-the-counter company in Mexico. It operates in more than 15 countries globally, including Europe and the Middle East. Its stock was placed into the IPC, the Mexican equivalent of the Dow Jones Industrial Average, and is the best-performing stock in the entire index.

Genomma Lab employs a number of amazingly creative processes to develop products and launch strategies in a fraction of the time their competition can. Then, by institutionalizing these unique processes, the company surges ahead of the competition with every move. They play on the fact that the competitions' organizational structure and standard practices, which they developed over decades, simply does not allow them to adopt Genomma Lab's most important business practices. I wish I could tell you about these brilliant processes, but like many outthinkers, Genomma Lab guards them carefully, so I cannot disclose them here. The important point to note is that Genomma Lab is winning because it understands that thinking about customer needs is not enough. Yes, you need to excel at finding and meeting customer needs. But to win over the long term, you also need to excel at understanding the competition and adopting a disruptive mind-set that allows you to continually keep ahead. Frankly, I think competing with Genomma Lab must be exhausting.

Slow Down the Competition

History is littered with stories of innovators with empty hands, their creations stolen by the competition. TiVo, for example, revolutionized television viewing by introducing the world to the digital video recorder (DVR)—only to have their innovation swept aside by cable companies who realized they could bundle their own DVRs into cable boxes and give them away for free (because DVR users invariably upgraded to a higher-priced cable package). Vonage, with great effort and expense, woke consumers up to the potential of Internet phones (voice over IP [VoIP]) only to have cable companies, again, bundle in their own VoIP offerings into cable service. Netflix, as we discussed already, may be headed toward a similar fate.

There is nothing wrong with creating a great product that inspires copycats. This is one way to transform an industry. Indeed, this is precisely how Muhammad Yunus brought microfinance to the poorest corners of the world. But to also *own* your innovation, you must step into the competitor's mind and ask yourself, "How would I copy that?"; then pick the ideas for which there is no good answer.

The interactive promotions company ePrize has found a creative way to do just that, but right now its people are dealing with an emergency. They are under siege by a group of attackers, dressed in gorilla costumes, from their archrival, Slither Corp. Slither personnel have entered ePrize's building, trying to find the keys to ePrize's success.

This assault is perhaps not completely unexpected because Slither has launched aggressive PR and e-mail campaigns in the past. Its name and logo—which resembles Enron's—seem designed to invoke fear. No matter how far ahead ePrize gets, Slither is just steps behind and closing in fast.

Yet Slither Corp. does not really exist.

It is a competitor fabricated by ePrize's management to keep this innovative company on its toes and leaning forward. The goal is to keep ePrize's people thinking from the competitor's point of view and guaranteeing the continuation of ePrize's phenomenal growth.

Under the leadership of founder and CEO Josh Linkner, ePrize has emerged as the dominant interactive promotions company in the United States and beyond. The company has produced more than 5,000 interactive promotions across 36 countries. It designs and executes Internet promotions campaigns for clients such as Coca-Cola,

American Express, Gap, Procter & Gamble, Warner Bros., Dell, and Adidas.

When you log on to a website and punch in a code you found under a bottle cap, there is a good chance you are experiencing ePrize's work firsthand. The company works with three-quarters of the top 100 brands and has more than doubled in size in the past two years. Since its inception, ePrize has consistently produced about 40 percent annual revenue growth.

By asking its employees what they think their counterparts at Slither would do, Linkner says ePrize "creates a fun, safe opening for continual discussion about what the company could do better."[4] It also establishes a disruptive filter. With Slither standing over their shoulders, forcing ePrize's people to ask, "How would Slither respond?" ePrize has a better chance of launching ideas clients will love and that the competition will not copy.

It does not take much to step back and ask, "How will the competition respond?" For outthinkers, it's a matter of habit.

When I deliver my seminars I usually open with the promise that participants will create multiple strategic ideas the competition will resist copying. Invariably someone protests: "That's impossible. Anything I do the competition can do." It's an argument I hear often because most of what we learn about competitive strategy in business school and read in business journals is written for large companies who have already established scale. When you are large, you look to do things your competition *cannot* do. But while you are getting to the top, while you are growing, you must do things your competition *will* not do.

Doing What Your Competition Will Not Do

I had the opportunity to hear a lecture by Andrew W. Lo, the MIT economist known for his theory of adaptive markets. I had read a bit about him and his ideas, but as I sat in the back of the massive ballroom, behind rows and rows of people, I realized that he was talking about something we are starting to see pop up in other, seemingly unrelated domains.

Lo believes that our old model of the world is broken because it assumes that people and markets act rationally. Instead, according to the adaptive market hypothesis, people adapt their expectations. Their behaviors are driven by biology, not mathematics; by greed, not by a cold assessment of risk and reward. Essentially, it assumes the agents who drive market dynamics are humans, not machines.

The same is true for competition. The old model of business strategy said that companies act rationally, so the way to win was to do something that others cannot do. But the outthinkers we have covered here disrupted their markets not by doing what others can't do, but rather simply by doing what others will not do. Indeed, study the early emergence of any great company and you are likely to see the same pattern play out: their large incumbent competitor could, if it makes the right sacrifices, kill off the rising star with minimal effort; but the big defender chooses not to defend itself. As Mohandas Gandhi said, "First they ignore you, then they laugh at you."

In other words, the sources of advantage, the barriers that protect fast-growing companies, are cognitive. They are not the hard, sustainable advantages we read about in business school.

Doing What Your Competition Cannot Do

The strategy that gets you there is not the strategy that keeps you there. It was Walmart's focus on rural markets that enabled it to become the largest retailer in the United States, but it was its economies of scale that enabled it to maintain this advantage. Although Dell's *go direct* strategy pushed it above HP and IBM, it was an efficient, customizable supply chain that maintained its top position for so many years.

Typically, as we saw earlier, fast-growing companies beat their competitors by doing something their competitors choose not to copy, even though they could. Over time, however, competitors grow weary of losing and they get over the cognitive and social barriers that are stopping them from competing. Eventually the competition wakes up to your success, and you need to shift your advantage to something more permanent.

One of my favorite business school professors, Bruce Greenwald, suggests in his book *Competition Demystified* that there are just three proven ways to sustain your innovation over the long term:

1. *Achieve customer captivity.* This is Microsoft leveraging its Windows dominance or cable companies leveraging the fact that they have the only thick cable plugged into your house.
2. *Secure preferential access to resources.* This is De Beers owning diamond mines and L'Oreal issuing three times as many patents each year as the competition.
3. *Build meaningful economies of scale.* This is Walmart using its scale to achieve lower distribution costs.

We've seen that today's outthinkers seem to focus more on the first two and less on the third: economies of scale. There are two reasons for this: building scale is becoming more difficult, and the way companies do it is changing. We can no longer look to a bigger factory or a larger distribution machine as the answer. Our opportunities are more limited. But those who look beyond the obvious sources of the past can, with effort and time, still build a moat around their innovation. Google built a scale advantage by establishing the largest advertising platform; Facebook, the largest social network; and Apple, the largest app store. We cannot see or touch the walls of these defenses, but the competitive protection they provide is just as effective as that of a giant Ford Motors factory 50 years ago.

The outthinkers who are growing today are actively pursuing such permanent sources of advantage. From the beginning, they start laying the foundation for building longer-term advantages. They build a captive customer base, they begin establishing preferred access to key resources, and they seek to build scale. Ariba is seeking to assemble the largest platform of suppliers to corporations. Alibaba is seeking to build the largest network of Chinese and developing-world manufacturers.

Block the Competition

When I ask people to pick ideas their competitors will not copy, they often respond with disbelief. "We aren't big enough," they protest.

"How can we possibly do something competitors cannot copy?" What they mean is, We're not big enough yet to achieve a permanent advantage like customer captivity, economies of scale, or preferred access to resources—all the things you say we need. Then I point out that they've focused on the wrong part of the question. You do not need to do something your competitors *cannot* copy. It is enough to do something they *will* not copy. Either way, you advance uncontested.

This typically brings up another level of incredulity. "If I do something and customers like it and my competitors can copy it, they will. They're smart. They have the funding. Why wouldn't they copy me?"

To answer this question, I analyzed about 100 companies that decisively beat their competition (in terms of growth, profitability, and shareholder return) over a 10-year period. These were companies that had adopted successful strategies that competitors, for one reason or the other, did not copy quickly. I looked specifically at why their competitors did not respond effectively. I found 14 key reasons why the competition does not respond in time to an outthinker's innovation.

	Outthinkers' Strategy	**Competitors' Rationale for Not Responding**	**Example**	**Stratagem No.***
1	Do not fight the current battle; instead focus on preparing for the next one.	They are not competing with us (today).	Rosetta Stone focuses on replicating the "emersion," rather than the classroom, experience.	12
2	Partner with someone outside of our market or the typical partner set because we both benefit by winning together.	Their partner does not understand our industry, so they will not be successful.	Honda partners with bicycle company to create Hero Honda Motors Limited.	5

*Stratagem number corresponds with Appendix B.

(*continued*)

(*continued*)

	Outthinkers' Strategy	**Competitors' Rationale for Not Responding**	**Example**	**Stratagem No.***
3	Borrow access to your target and then, if possible, take over the partner that gave you access.	We are partners who share joint interests, so there is no reason to adopt a defensive stance.	Logitech first sells peripherals through PC manufacturers (later sells direct).	24
4	Be helpful/friendly to our would-be competitor; then (possibly) compete with them when we are in a sufficiently strong position.	They are helping us.	Google offers to outsource search for Yahoo!	33
5	Retreat from the current conflict in a way that positions us well for a future attack; attack later, possibly in a different location, when the time is right.	They are giving up.	Qualcomm exits handset business.	16 and 20
6	When lots of people are retreating, they are likely leaving behind opportunities, so we move in and pick off that which	The situation is too risky to advance; they are making a mistake.	Coca-Cola increases investment in countries in economic distress; Carlos Slim and Warren Buffet invest where	15

*Stratagem number corresponds with Appendix B.

	Outthinkers' Strategy	Competitors' Rationale for Not Responding	Example	Stratagem No.*
	is of value that they leave behind.		the market is retreating.	
7	They are expecting everyone to take one path to the customer, so we will take an unexpected one and they will not respond.	They will take the orthodox path, and (when they do not) the path they chose does not work.	Dell sells directly to consumers.	30
8	Establish a facade that appears to be our real business (X), then capture profits in a different, related business (Y).	They are in the X business, so we should compete with them there (thereby ignoring the Y business).	Thomson Travel appears to be travel retail business but pools profits in charter airline.	25
9	If we take a subservient stance today, they will accept us; we can later build power and take control.	They are not seeking control, so are not a threat to us.	Intel convinces IBM to build the PC around the Intel chip.	23
10	Launch a small attack to see how the competition/ market will respond; then launch our real attack with this information.	They are not fully committed to winning (or are not capable of winning), so there is no reason for us to take them seriously.	Microsoft enters into web browser and server markets.	14
11	If we combine small things into bigger things (e.g., bundle	They are offering something different from	Microsoft's strategy of bundling	9

*Stratagem number corresponds with Appendix B.

(*continued*)

(continued)

	Outthinkers' Strategy	Competitors' Rationale for Not Responding	Example	Stratagem No.*
	products) or separate things into smaller things, the competition will not see us as a competitor.	what we are offering; this is not a comparable product or service	mutliple programs in the Office Suite.	
12	We will use a model, idea, or technology they have abandoned; because they have invested in its more advanced alternative, they will resist reembracing what they abandoned.	Either (1) they are using an outdated model, idea, or technology, or (2) it is too expensive for us to go back.	RIM built the original BlackBerry on abandoned pager text networks.	27
13	Appear to be making a decision based on faulty logic so that others will not take us seriously.	They have not thought through what they are doing; it will not work.	Virgin's Richard Branson entered into the airline and other businesses.	18
14	This is an opportunity that the competition will not want to take advantage of because pursuing it would damage one of their other business.	That opportunity is not for us because it will cost us too much (in another business) to pursue it.	Apple released the iPod while Sony resisted using the Walkman to allow easy digital music distribution.	17

*Stratagem number corresponds with Appendix B.

Conclusion

If everything eventually becomes a toaster, the job of the outthinker is twofold. First, you must figure out how to slow down that process as much as possible. This means convincing the competition to hold off copying you, even if they can. The longer you can hold them off, the longer you have to be earning a higher profit margin. Second, you must always be moving so nimbly that your competitors can't copy you, even if they want to.

CHAPTER 12

Shaping Perceptions

Reality is merely an illusion. Albeit a persistent one.

—Albert Einstein[1]

The art of moving people's wills involves more skill than determination. You must know how to get inside the other person. . . . Everyone idolizes something. Some want to be well thought of, others idolize profit, and most people idolize pleasure. The trick is to identify the idols that can set people in motion.

—Balthasar Gracian, *The Art of Worldly Wisdom*, Chapter 26[2]

Elon Musk, the chief executive officer (CEO) of Tesla Motors, knew they were in trouble. They had solved the technical challenges of building a purely electric high-performance car. Their battery technology, in particular, was arguably the best in the world. They already had cars on the road that were getting great reviews. But the company was running out of cash. If they couldn't find someone willing to inject several million dollars into the company, all their work might have been for naught. So when Musk got the news that Daimler was coming to town to talk about some kind of relationship, his first reaction was elation.

The team only had two weeks to prepare. Musk first called his head of engineering and asked if they could conceivably convert a Daimler Smart car into an electric one in time. Yes, it would be possible—but they would have to drop everything else to do it.

Musk sent one of the team members to purchase a Daimler Smart car—no small feat given that the Smart car was not yet available in the United States. Undaunted, Musk instructed the Tesla's finance department to hand his team member a backpack filled with $20,000 in cash and sent him to Mexico to make the purchase. With the Smart car secured and back at Tesla headquarters in California, the engineering team worked nonstop, day and night, for 10 days to outfit the Smart car with Tesla electric car innards.

On cue, the Daimler team arrived, led by a senior executive who seemed too serious to smile. Musk brought them to the board room and began his presentation, explaining the relative performance of Tesla's technology. But in the middle of his presentation, he could tell the Daimler team was not engaging, so Musk changed his approach. He abruptly stopped the presentation and invited the Daimler team to see a surprise. They walked down to the Tesla garage, a converted airplane hangar, and Musk opened the doors to reveal a Smart car. The Daimler team was not impressed. They had seen Smart cars before.

But when Musk explained this was an *electric* Smart car, the Daimler team was shocked. Daimler didn't make an electric Smart car. And since Tesla's engineering team had been careful not to alter the car's exterior or cockpit, it was difficult to see the difference. "No," Musk insisted, "this really is an electric car. Want to try it out?" With that, he and the head of the Daimler team, the one who seemed never to smile, climbed in.

Musk sat in the driver's seat and hit the accelerator. The power of the massive Tesla engine turning inside the tiny, light Smart car lurched the car forward—Tesla's engines are, after all, designed for a sports car that accelerates as fast as a Porsche. The front wheels came off the ground, and Musk and his guest were gone, speeding around Tesla's property.

Fifteen minutes later, the Daimler executive climbed out of the car—smiling.

Two weeks later Daimler announced it would invest $50 million in Tesla Motors. That was followed by a similar investment from Toyota and an IPO. Tesla was saved.

Darryl Siry, Tesla's former vice president of sales and marketing, said this about Musk: "It's a reality distortion field and it's a powerful one. He gives the facts to fit the narrative he wants out there." I think Musk—and all successful innovators—are necessarily reality twisters. Those who worked with Steve Jobs describe the same "reality distortion field" following him around. Muhammad Yunus, a Nobel Peace Prize winner and creator of microcredit, says that his greatest challenge has been "to change the mindsets of people."[3] The entrepreneur and TV news personality Donny Deutsch repeats a simple but profound statement that entrepreneurs need to embrace: "Fake it till you make it." The greatest challenge, in other words, is convincing other people to believe in your innovation.

Outthinkers change the world because they are skilled at shaping others' perceptions, building buy-in for their ideas. Musk, for example, had to convince not only Daimler and Toyota but also early investors, employees, and later shareholders that Tesla was going to work. He had to convince regulators and elected officials to maintain incentives for people to buy and develop electric vehicles. If you cannot pull together the conviction of the stakeholders who need to realize your idea, you have made little impact on the world.

As we noted in Chapter 7, many of the things we create today—products, services, and companies—are social constructions. They exist because people agree they exist. A dollar is worth a dollar because we all agree it is. Microfinance has transformed the lives of millions of poor people because Yunus convinced enough people that microfinance exists. Apple is an aspirational company only because enough people say it is. As the expressionist artist Louise Nevelson said, "What we call reality is an agreement that people have arrived at to make life more livable."[4] This is critical—it puts the ability to shape others' perceptions at the heart of outthinking.

To change the world, you need to change reality, and to change reality you need to change perception, which you engineer with creative language. First, you need to create a compelling idea. It works best if you describe an ideal situation that appeals to people's common sense—and keep it very simple. Then you need to diagnose the changes that need to take place. For bold ideas to be realized, it usually requires that multiple parts of the system undergo radical change.

Musk's vision of an electric car that could travel halfway across the country on one charge between breakfast and bedtime requires not only breakthroughs in battery technology but also the creation of a system of service stations where drivers can swap out batteries. It requires the passing of new laws and regulations to encourage electric vehicles. It's a multifaceted problem that seems impossible if you view these challenges as reasons the idea won't work. But if you view them as variables in the system that you can influence, then they simply become part of the puzzle.

Finally, you need to explore possible solutions, including ideas that have never been tried before. The breakthrough usually occurs through an analogy or metaphor. Yunus, for example, banged his head against the banking sector, which refused to accept his idea of microcredit. His dream became reality when he stopped viewing his project as a social plan but rather as a bank for the poor. Then all of the previously insurmountable problems revealed simple solutions.

These three steps—create the idea, diagnose the necessary changes, and explore solutions—are the beginning of the Outthinker Process that we will examine in detail in Chapters 13 to 17.

■ ■ ■

In December 2009, James Cameron's three-dimensional (3D) movie *Avatar* broke a historic barrier by becoming the highest-grossing film of all time. It even beat out Cameron's own *Titanic*. The story of how Cameron engineered this feat offers a valuable lesson for anyone wishing to impact the world. If you want to build a business, launch a product, or drive social change, Cameron's journey points to a tool set that all successful innovators use to overcome the fundamental challenge of innovation.

That fundamental challenge is this: All innovations begin with a new vision that is inconsistent with current reality. Successful innovators are able to enroll a critical mass of people in that vision so that it actually becomes reality. I call this the *formation process*. It is like creating a pointillistic painting. You know what you want to create (your vision), but to make it real you must carefully place dot after dot on the canvas until the world recognizes your vision. Each dot represents a stakeholder that you must enroll.

A January 2010 cover story in *BusinessWeek* nicely plots out Cameron's journey. In summary, it shows that for Cameron's big vision to be real, he would need to enroll four stakeholders: (1) he'd have to convince a massive number of moviegoers to pay 30 percent premiums for renting 3D glasses, (2) he'd have to convince movie theaters to upgrade their equipment, (3) he'd have to convince camera companies to improve 3D video technology, and (4) he'd have to convince a studio to fund it all. Each stakeholder had reasons to support his vision and reasons to resist it. Great innovators know how to elevate the former and alleviate the latter.

There isn't space here to walk through how Cameron skillfully untangled that which was causing resistance in each stakeholder, but for illustrative purposes, let's look at #4, the movie studios. Fox had the right of first refusal, so Cameron was determined to find a way to get them to fund the project at an anticipated cost of $200 million. Fox was hesitant; this would be one of the most expensive movies ever made, and they feared he would go over this budget, just as he had with *Titanic*.

To bring Fox into the fold, Cameron used a number of tactics. Of course, he started with a compelling vision and an eye-catching sample film clip. These are tools all good directors can employ. But when these tactics did not distinguish Cameron's innovative skill or convince Fox, Cameron went further than the average director would think to.

First, he addressed Fox's concern about technology by investing his own money, about $12 million, in developing a camera rig that could capture two-dimensional (2D) and 3D imagery simultaneously. Second, when Fox looked like it was going to say "no," he approached Disney. Disney's interest brought Fox more firmly to the table. Third, to reduce Fox's financial risk, Cameron helped arrange the support of a London-based private equity firm, Ingenious Media, which in the past 10 years had raised $8 billion to invest in films. With the technology in place, a credible threat in the wings, and someone willing to absorb more than half the risk, Fox green-lighted *Avatar*.

Cameron's journey was touch and go. He hit dead ends that would have discouraged many of us and made us simply give in. Like all successful innovators I've interviewed, though, he persisted, confident in the value of his vision, painstakingly forcing the dots into place until the painting's image became evident to everyone. Innovators like Cameron all realize that the most important perspective is one that clearly illustrates how everyone will benefit from their vision.

In his January 2011 State of the Union speech, President Obama spoke of "out-innovating" the competition. But to focus on his agenda of clean energy and education is to miss a subtle insight into Obama's skill as an innovator. You see, Obama knows a secret. Steve Jobs knew it, too, and so do Muhammad Yunus (grandfather of microcredit), Elon Musk (chief executive officer [CEO] of Tesla Motors), and anyone else who has proved that he or she is capable of driving significant innovations into the world.

The secret is this: people don't think; they react. Innovators know how to use this to their advantage, by linking the facts to the right stories—the stories that trigger the responses they want to see in others.

While writing my last book, *The Way of Innovation*, I came across a fascinating experiment that illustrates this point. Cognitive scientists studied how babies reacted to a popped balloon. The first time a balloon pops, a baby does not respond. But after hearing a balloon pop enough times, the baby starts showing signs of being startled. By the time of adulthood, the person responds to the sound immediately and unconsciously. People act without thinking. Indeed, academics estimate that 94 percent of our actions are driven by subconscious thought. We hear a balloon pop; we flinch.

What innovators know is that it is far more difficult to reprogram someone's response to a popping balloon than it is to show that no balloon is popping.

Let's start with Steve Jobs and Apple. In January 2011 Apple made two big announcements: Jobs was taking a permanent leave of absence and Apple's fourth-quarter profits had increased 78 percent from the prior year. There are two ways these facts could have been released and two different triggered responses:

1. *Profits first:* "Apple profits soar" [but] "Steve Jobs is leaving" would have startled the market like a popped balloon. It would have led to stories about a successful company now losing its leader.
2. *Profits second:* "Steve Jobs is leaving" [but] "Apple profits soar" avoids startling the market. It leads to stories about Apple maintaining performance despite Jobs' leaving.

How the market reacts has less to do with the facts (Jobs was overseeing Apple for more than 360 of the 365 days during which Apple produced its annual revenue growth) and everything to do with the story that investors start telling themselves when they hear the facts.

Obama gets this. He could have made an argument—as too many business gurus do—about the world changing, about our entering an uncharted era. Instead, he reached back to the past and argued that our country is reliving the Sputnik moment, when the USSR beat us into space. He strategically chose to pop the balloon that triggers the response he desires: the United States waking up to the challenge and out-innovating the threat.

Listen to enough great innovators talk, and you will see a pattern. They rarely argue that we are entering an entirely new world. To do so is to give up control over how people will respond. Who knows what will happen in a new world? Instead, they influence our response by activating a story we know; they suggest that we are reliving something we already have successfully responded to. They think carefully about which balloon to pop, keeping in mind how we will react. The best communicators are the ones who can create and share a strong narrative story. The best novels are the ones with the most compelling plot, and the best speeches are the ones that arouse an emotional response from a crowd.

We also see the use of narratives in the business world. A company's narrative has shown itself to be a key tool in building a thriving business and getting people excited about a new idea. Great companies are all using a narrative to keep their stakeholders interested and dedicated. That's why the best business leaders are also great storytellers. People relate to stories because they are part of their evolutionary makeup.

When humans first started to communicate with one another, they did so by sharing stories. They kept their history and traditions alive by spinning a tale to connect a sequence of events. Stories are how we learn. As the neuroscientist Marco Iacoboni, whom we met in Chapter 6, explains, "Early on in life we learn a lot of things through stories. As a child you listen to your parents and teachers and you learn lessons from their stories about right and wrong. When you go to bed, you are told stories. There is something almost primal about our evolution and development that leads us back to listening to stories."[5]

The mirror neurons Iacoboni describes help us see why narratives are so powerful. He conducted an experiment in which he showed people pictures that morphed together an image of themselves and one of their friends. Some pictures were more like the observer, and some were more like the friend. Then Iacoboni measured mirror neuron activity and found that when the picture looked more like the observer, the observer's mirror neurons fired more strongly.

In other words, the more people see themselves in the picture, the more their mirror neurons fire. The more people see themselves in you, the more they relate to you. They think, "This person is like me," and since most of us like ourselves, they think, "I like this person."

Highly influential people tell stories that spark mirror neurons in others by opening their stories with images, sounds, smells, and feelings that others recognize and can relate to. As Iacoboni says, "Innovators create stories that others want to be part of."[6]

At the Democratic National Convention in 2004, then-Senator Barack Obama created a story of solidarity, or hope, that many

Americans got behind. His narrative sparked millions of mirror neurons when he said:

> *There's not a liberal America and a conservative America; there's the United States of America. There's not a black America and white America and Latino America and Asian America; there's the United States of America.*

Obama tapped into the empathy of his audiences because he was able to build an idea that people could see, touch, and feel.

Conclusion

The final habit that outthinkers exhibit is shaping perceptions. We often think the job ends when we have come up with the brilliant idea. What is left is to simply execute it. But before you even have something to execute, you must enroll key stakeholders—funders, employees, partners, and so on. This requires shifting their perspectives so that they see the attractiveness of your idea.

The key difference between how outthinkers take on this challenge and how less skilled influencers operate is that outthinkers get into the minds of those they are seeking to influence. They shift their language—their metaphors, narratives, and frames—and pick precisely the right words. They understand that reality is relative, that very little of the reality we operate in is rooted in hard, tangible fact. They shape others' perceptions and in doing so shape their realities and change the world.

PART 4

Apply the Outthinker Process

Some 500 years ago, Niccoló Machiavelli was one of the first to point out innovation's fundamental challenge:

There is nothing more difficult to take in hand, more perilous to conduct, than to take a lead in the introduction of a new order of things, because the innovation has for enemies all those who have done well under the old conditions and lukewarm defenders in those who may do well under the new.

The Outthinker Process, described in the next five chapters, is a program I developed in an attempt to solve that challenge—to convert innovation's enemies and energize its lukewarm supporters. This has been the focus of my professional life for the past 10 years. In that time my colleagues and I have trained several thousand people in the process, from employees at companies such as Microsoft, General Electric, L'Oreal, Johnson & Johnson, Symantec, and Walmart, as well as a long roster of fast-growing mid-market companies. We now train about 2,000 people each year.

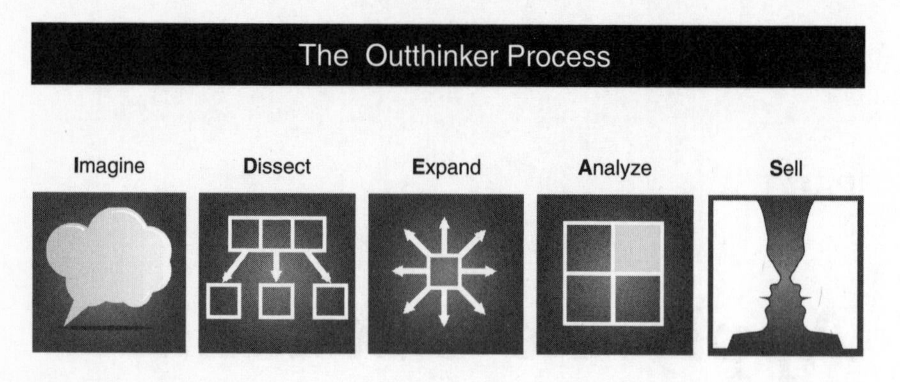

You can apply the Outtinker Process individually or in a group, to tackle small or large problems. This section describes how to apply the process in a group. But whether you are using it to facilitate your entire team through a three-day strategy off-site or whether you are in a taxi planning for fifteen minutes in your notebook before your next meeting, the steps and tools are the same.

I Start Each Workshop with Three Promises

1. You will see new strategic options for solving a real challenge you face today, and you will be excited by the possibilities these options give you.
2. You will reach strategic clarity, having defined a game plan composed of a few priorities you can immediately begin executing or validating.
3. You will begin developing new strategic thinking habits.

I make you the same promise.

I don't pretend that the process is magic. But because I have seen it applied so many times, with such success, I can say without hesitation that it works. I know that it helps develop the five habits described in Part 3 of this book. I know that managers who apply it consistently see exciting new possibilities for solving real challenges. I know that when a group of people begins adopting the process, it can actually bring about a shift in culture, where innovative thinking is no longer confined to one department but becomes part of the company's normal atmosphere.

For example, I began applying a version of the process at Microsoft about five years ago. At the time, many thought Microsoft was losing its innovative edge. My colleagues and I have had an opportunity to work with several hundred of Microsoft's emerging high-potential leaders each year. We found that managers who really embraced the Outthinker Process experienced a shift in how they worked together. They are more comfortable exploring crazy ideas, less likely to immediately kill off ideas that may seem unorthodox, and are able to more effectively share these ideas with colleagues in the company. Now, of course, our effort is but one small piece of a broad effort, driven by many top leaders, composed of numerous initiatives, to drive innovative thinking in the company. And, of course, Microsoft's future remains unwritten, but we are beginning to see real evidence that some forward-looking strategic choices are starting to pay off with new devices, acquisitions, and strategic moves.

The process works on both large and small problems. As long as you have a goal and want a better way to achieve it, the Outthinker Process can help. It is, however, best suited for problems that are strategic in nature. It has been used, for instance, to develop breakthrough strategies for solving issues such as these:

- How do we win this next key account?
- How can we triple our growth rate in the next three years?
- How do we double customer satisfaction?
- Who can we acquire to leap-frog the competition?

The Outthinker Process does not deliver prepackaged solutions. What it does do is enable its users to rapidly generate unorthodox strategic options and begin creating a new context inside the company that encourages more innovative strategic thinking. When that becomes your organization's standard way of thinking, there is no limit to what you can achieve.

CHAPTER 13

Step 1 Imagine

Imagination is the beginning of creation. You imagine what you desire, you will what you imagine and at last you create what you will.

—George Bernard Shaw[1]

Forethought we may have, undoubtedly, but not foresight.

—Napoleon Bonaparte[2]

A famous Taoist story, by the ancient Chinese philosopher Chuang Tzu, tells of a farmer whose horse has run away. All the townspeople console him, saying, "What bad luck." But the farmer replies, "Who knows, maybe this is good news." A few weeks later, the horse returns and brings along another horse of excellent breeding. Everyone congratulates the farmer, but he says, "How do you know this is not bad news?" Sometime later, his son falls from a horse and breaks his leg. His neighbors come again to console him and he says, "This may be good luck." A war breaks out and the emperor drafts all able-bodied young men into the army, but since the farmer's son is injured, he is spared. His neighbors say, "What good luck!" and the farmer says, "How do you know?"

The lesson here is that the neighbors are shortsighted. They take short-term news, project it into the future, and each time think that the whole world has changed.

Companies that win over the long term think like that farmer. They ingest short-term news in moderation while remaining focused on their long-term strategy. Chuang Tzu knew this, Warren Buffett does, and you probably do, too.

But daily dramas are so tempting.

Envision the Future

Think back to the story of Rosetta Stone in Chapter 3. This innovative language software company issued one of the hottest IPOs of 2009 and in the process became the darling of Wall Street. Yet 10 years earlier the company was effectively unknown. How did they emerge from obscurity to dominance? By imagining a new future and putting in place a strategy that would get them there.

Rosetta Stone, you might remember, envisioned a future in which instead of moving to Italy for a few months to learn Italian, you could replicate that experience at home. Every key strategic decision followed from that vision. To realize it meant dismantling and replacing the business strategy. It meant raising prices by 1,000 percent, shifting distribution from bookstores to kiosks, changing hiring practices to include fewer learning experts and more people who have learned a second language naturally, and building a product that replaced verb conjugation and vocabulary memorization with visual pattern matching games. Every one of those decisions probably seemed crazy to outsiders, yet each was critical to making the future vision a reality. And the results were stunning.

This ability to envision a new future, one inconsistent with current reality, and hold it your mind is something we can all develop. It is more a habit than a skill. And it is a critical habit for anyone who wants to change the world. Because, as Leland Stanford Sr. said, "A man will never construct anything he cannot conceive."[3]

> Directing a film is not that dissimilar to being the creative director of a large fashion house. First of all, you have to have a vision; that's the most important thing.
>
> —*Tom Ford, director of* A Single Man, *and former creative director at Gucci*[4]

Practice Mental Time Travel

The ability to mentally travel forward in time is a critical tool. It allows us to prepare for potential future events and adapt to uncertainty, both of which provide an advantage for us individually and for our companies.

Scientists have shown, however, that the process of mental time travel is different from what we might think. When people imagine the future, they are not creating a new future in their mind; rather, they are piecing together past memories to create a collage of a possible new future. What we are able to imagine, then, is limited by the breadth of our past memories, by our ability to access and manipulate them, and by our ability to focus our attention.

To overcome these limitations, you might consider gathering together a team of people to explicitly and collaboratively describe your desired future. This gives you access to a much broader catalog of memories (those of your colleagues) and helps avoid distractions.

The Exercise

Having conducted some 500 workshops, I have found that the best way to proceed is to focus the discussion on three dimensions: (1) you and your organization, (2) the relevant environment that affects your company, and (3) the other players, such as competitors, regulators, suppliers, and distributors. Gather your team and guide them through the following three steps:

1. Define the mess.

   For your team to be willing to consider alternative futures, they must first grow sufficiently discontented with the current trajectory. You have probably witnessed meetings in which someone acts bored, failing to see that what you are working on is worth the time. This person thinks, "What we're doing is fine." Until you get everyone to accept that it is worth finding a better way today, you will extract only a small portion of the team's intelligence.

   So start out by having people discuss what the future would be like if things went wrong. This should be a realistic possibility, not a disaster. For example, a client in the leasing business was discussing its goal of being number one. It became apparent that although their revenues were growing, they were growing only as fast as the market, so they were not gaining market share. It slowly dawned on everyone in the room that if they did not do something different, they would always be just one of many players. This discontent woke them up and put them into a state of urgency.

2. Define the long-term ideal.

   This next step should feel like lifting your gaze off your feet and looking out at the horizon. Your team, given the chance to dream, should be left inspired. Perhaps they will feel a little scared, unsure if the long-term ideal really is feasible, but they will be excited about playing to win that game.

   This step has three parts.

   a. Decide how you want to define *long term*. This typically means three to five years from now, but it could be as soon as next year or as far away as the next decade. In my workshops, I often use Tesla Motors, a company introduced in Chapter 8, as a practice case. For Tesla we define the long term as five years from now.
   b. Imagine your long-term ideal. You will need to take several questions into account.

      What ideal state do you hope for? What are your values? Your mission? What vision are you pursuing?

      What will the environment be like at that time?

      What will the other players be doing?

      It is important to complete this step in the order listed here—first you, then the environment, then the others. Many people like to start with the environment, asking, for example, "What new trends do we want to take advantage of?" This is the process advocated by scenario planning. Although it may seem logical, I find it tends to lead to reactive, *me-too* decisions.

      Outthinkers come at it from a different direction. "Regardless of what is going on in the world, we are going to achieve our mission. So what is that mission?" *After* they have defined what they and their organization want, they look at the environment they must work within and the players they will have to contend with.

Returning to the Tesla case, in my workshops, participants usually describe Tesla's long-term vision as something like this: "Tesla has triggered a change in the car market. Electric vehicles are being launched, and price points are much lower today, approaching the price everyday drivers can afford. Most cars use Tesla technology even if Tesla does not produce the car on its own." Then they discuss the environment, noting that oil prices are high today but could drop dramatically, that growing conflict in oil-producing countries is creating increased urgency to reduce dependency on oil, and that automobile traffic in developing countries is expected to explode. Finally they move on to the other players, particularly key competitors and legislatures with the power to introduce consumer credits.

c. Complete the process by defining up to three key metrics that capture your long-term ideal. These may be external numbers, such as revenue and market share; internal numbers, such as employee engagement or efficiency; or personal metrics, such as your salary or how many times per week you get home in time to put your children to sleep. For the Tesla case, participants often settle on something like "in five years: (a) the number of electric vehicles sold in the world should grow five times or more and (b) the portion of them that use Tesla technology should be 40 percent."

   At the end of this three-phase process of defining the long-term ideal, you and your team should share a common vision for a compelling future you are all excited about. It is grounded in a reasonably deep understanding of what is going on the world—how the environment will change and what other players will be doing.

3. Define your near-term ideal.
   a. Decide how far ahead you want to define as the *near term*. Make it close enough that it's relevant, yet far out enough that you can actually make something happen between now and then. If it takes you 12 months to launch a new product, for example, you don't want to pick a period shorter than a year, because doing so would kill off new product ideas. In most cases the near term is between six months and three years. For the Tesla case, participants usually choose three years.
   b. Ask yourself, "What must be true in the near term for us to know we will realize our long-term ideal?" You may find, for example,

that to achieve your long-term vision, you have to acquire a certain amount of resources, your organization will have to build certain capabilities, or the regulators will have to have changed the rules. Discuss and note in short bulleted form what must be true. For the Tesla case, participants often list things like, "We must have a well-known brand;" "We must be financially stable (otherwise large car companies will not want to depend on us a vendor);" and "We must have the best battery technology in the world."

   c. Define the key metrics that capture your near-term ideal. These are often the same metrics you used for your long-term ideal, but they may differ. To reach your long-term revenue growth number, for example, you may decide you first need to focus on customer satisfaction over the near term. For the Tesla case, participants usually stick with the same metrics they defined in the long-term. They assume that to end up with a 40 percent share of electric vehicles that use Tesla technology, the company will have to start with something higher and that this makes sense since right now Tesla has less competition than it is likely to have in five years.

4. State your strategic question:
   a. Step back and consider the near-term ideal you and your team have discussed, looking particularly at the metrics.
   b. Now state your strategic question. This question, once answered, should lead you to achieving your near-term ideal. It should be specific, measurable (i.e., your key metrics should be part of the question), and bounded by time (e.g., "In 12 months, how do we . . . ?"). The strategic question participants set for the Tesla case usually is some version of "How do we help double the number of electric vehicles sold in the world and ensure that 80 percent of them use Tesla technology in three years?"

Hopefully after completing this first step, your team members feel excited and energized as they look at a clear, compelling strategic question and know that by answering that question they will set themselves on a trajectory to achieve their dreams. But your long-term ideal may appear difficult to achieve, and some members of your team may feel disheartened. Remind yourself that the only reason the problem seems unsolvable is that you do not have a solution yet, and this is also precisely why it's worth spending the time finding a solution.

CHAPTER 14

Step 2 Dissect

When Simplicity is broken up, It is made into instruments. . . . In this way, the Great System is united.

—Lao Tzu, *The Tao Te Ching*, Verse 28[1]

With your vision firmly in mind, the next step is to dissect your challenge into its component parts. We suggest doing this by building a system map that outlines the causes and effects and the variables and their dependencies so that you can understand how changes in one variable affect others. There are two advantages for doing this:

1. You may see a new leverage point. This could be an important variable, one that affects the game, but one that you have not considered before and that your competition is not considering. It opens up new solution space, creating the potential for you to do things no one else is expecting
2. You may narrow the scope of the problem. You may find that many parts of the problem are already solved and that you will get the best yield on your time and creativity by focusing on just one or a few issues.

CASE EXAMPLE: RIM FINDS A NEW LEVERAGE POINT

When two Canadian engineers decided to enter the U.S. market for mobile devices, they brought with them few competitive advantages. There was no reason to expect that without access to loyal customers, without any scale advantages, and with little existing proprietary technology to speak of, they would eventually build a company that would offer the most popular smartphone in the world.

But Mike Lazaridis and Jim Balsillie and their company, Research in Motion, saw something that others had overlooked. They saw that as telecom companies and mobile device manufacturers were advancing technology, moving from simple text-based pagers toward the dream of offering a mobile phone that could deliver text, voice, Internet, and even video content, they were forgetting something.

They were abandoning the network of transmission towers and related infrastructure already in place to deliver text data to pagers. There was significant excess capacity for anyone who wanted to deliver text pages. So, the entrepreneurs approached BellSouth and offered to build a two-way text pager and then developed new technology that enabled them to use the existing text network. Research in Motion was the only company offering a device on the old platform. Although their device lacked the bells and whistles of more modern offerings—for example, users couldn't have a voice conversation—it did prove to be unique. Competitors had nothing like it and, more important, no interest in trying to compete. They had, after all, abandoned the old text network.

The conclusion of this case is now well known. RIM's ugly, bulky two-way pager device evolved into the BlackBerry, which, at the time of writing, commands a 35 percent market share, making it the most popular smartphone in the world.

Whether RIM can retain its market share is perhaps in question. But the fact that two engineers from Canada could build such a large and successful company and have a hand in transforming an industry, indeed transforming the lives of billions of people around the world, points to the power of being able to see the big picture and seeing variables (in this case, the abandoned text network) that the other players have overlooked.

Analyze the System

To help you and your team to see the big picture and identify points of leverage or variables that others are overlooking, it helps to build a systems map. It's simple to do. First, restate, in summarized form, your near-term ideal in a small box in the middle of a piece of paper. Then ask yourself what needs to be true for you to achieve this near-term ideal.

Think carefully about the specific requirements or the specific drivers that have an effect, and write them down in boxes around this center box. Use arrows to connect the boxes and indicate the direction of the influence. This should give you a diagram with one box in the middle, representing your near-term ideal, surrounded by three to five key drivers or requirements.

Study these key drivers and choose the ones that seem to be most critical. You may find that some variables are already taken care of, or will be with time. You may already have easy solutions to solve other variables. This leaves a limited number of key variables for which you need to find solutions.

Systems Map Example

As a fun example, pretend that you and your team have decided that you want to rob a bank. In the center of your page, draw a square, and in that square, write "rob a bank." Then ask yourself what needs to be true in order for us to successfully achieve this near-term vision. You may decide on four things:

1. You need to get to the bank.
2. You need to get into the bank.
3. You need to get the money.
4. You need to get home safely without being caught.

Try to make your model simple, yet complete. You should feel confident that if you can achieve everything listed, you will achieve your goal. In this example, if you can get to the bank and get inside, collect the money, and get home safely without being caught, it seems that you will have successfully robbed the bank.

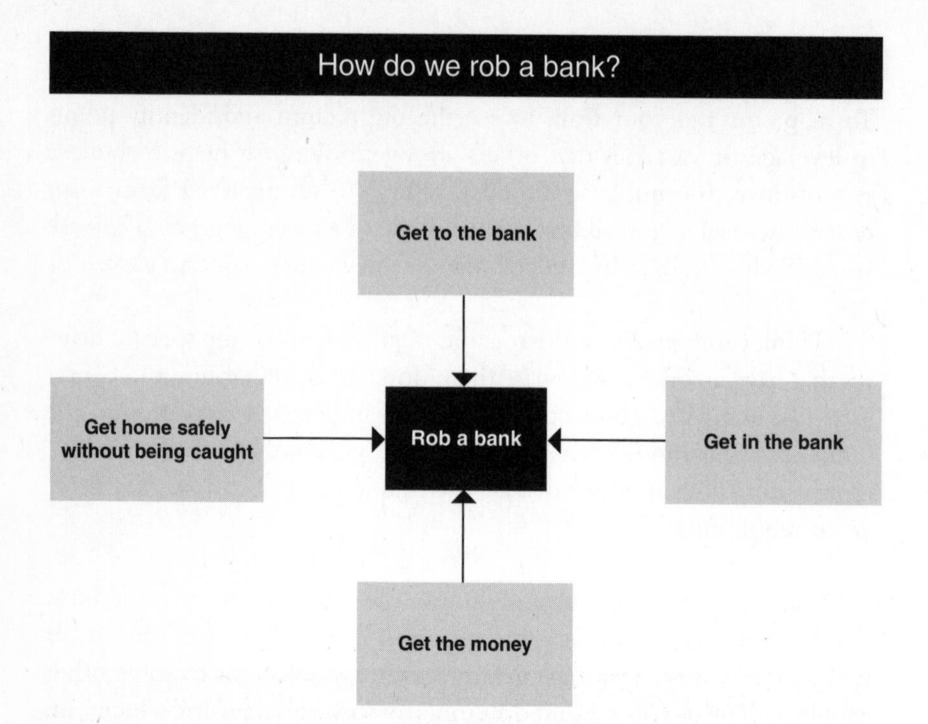

To make sure that your model is complete, it helps to imagine that you are about to deliver your presentation to a senior executive. At the beginning of your presentation, you outline your model. You say, for example, "We asked ourselves, 'How can we rob a bank?' and we decided that if we could do A, B, C, and D, we would be able to rob the bank." If you believe that the smart but skeptical senior executive would listen to the opening of your presentation and feel confident that you have covered everything, that you have not overlooked an important area of the problem and are ready to move forward.

At McKinsey & Company, I was trained through constant repetition to break problems down into mutually exclusive, collectively exhaustive (MECE) components. This term is fundamental at the firm, where *everything* is presented and analyzed in an MECE way. After a while you get so used to thinking in MECE ways that you even break grocery lists and weekend chores into MECE pieces.

This term is helpful in building out a systems map. If you can make sure that at each note of your map—the boxes coming out of it—is mutually exclusive (there is no overlap between them, nothing would fit into more than one box) and collectively exhaustive (there can be no other box that you have not yet thought about), then you reduce the chance of missing something. Your analysis is far more rigorous.

If you have more than seven boxes with arrows pointing at your near-term aspiration, then you are probably being overly complex. It is likely that some of those boxes should actually have arrows pointing at other boxes. That is, they are not primary drivers; they are secondary drivers.

Once you have your primary drivers listed, you can then begin to further expand your systems map. Pick one of the primary drivers that you think is important for the team to work on and continue expanding the map. Ask yourself, "What are the secondary drivers that influence this primary driver?" Repeat this for every primary driver to which you would like to find the answer.

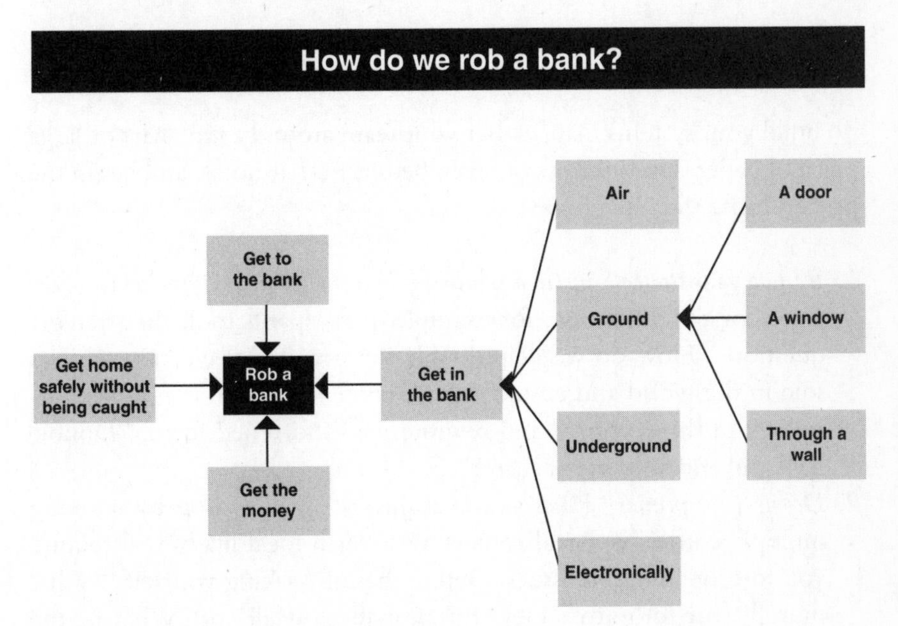

In our example, we might decide to first focus on how to get into the bank. We may decide that there are four ways to do it: by air, at ground level, underground, or electronically. We may then decide to take a deeper look at the ground option and discuss the options for getting in at the ground level: through a door, through a window, or through a wall.

Continue the process until you have expanded your systems map to the point that you feel that you have achieved some new insight. The goal is not to create a complete and accurate depiction of the system. That's probably impossible; and even if possible, it's of little use. A systems map that accurately describes the system for something as simple as ordering a bottle of wine would be too complex and too large to be of any practical value.

This exercise has two goals: (1) to help your team to expand its point of view and thereby begin seeing new leverage points that your competition is overlooking and (2) to find an opportunity to narrow the scope of the problem, focusing on the parts with the potential to generate the greatest return on your effort.

The Exercise

To build your systems map, gather your team around a flip chart or large piece of paper. Use markers or, even better, Post-it notes, and begin the process using the form here:

1. *Restate your strategic question, writing it in a small square at the center of the page.* For the Tesla case, for example, participants took the strategic question, "How do we help double the number of electric vehicles sold in the world and ensure that 80 percent of them use Tesla technology in three years?" and rewrote it in shortened form: "Double EVs sold and 80 percent share?"
2. *Define your primary issues or drivers.* Just as a war is won by winning multiple battles, you realize your near-term ideal likely will require you to solve multiple issues. Define these by asking yourself, "What must be true for us to achieve this near-term ideal?" or "What are the issues that we have to consider to fully address our strategic question?" Write each primary variable in a small square around the strategic question and use arrows to connect each to your near-term ideal and indicate the direction of influence. For the Tesla case, participants might break down the problem into three pieces: technology, cars, and drivers. The rationale for this breakdown is that as long we can

get our technology into enough EV cars and get drivers to buy them, we can double EVs sold and achieve an 80 percent share.

3. *Selectively expand the map.* Pick one primary issue you want your team to attack. If you already have a solution for that issue, leave it untouched on the map. If it calls out to you as something that appears particularly important and difficult to solve, it is probably worth spending time to further dissect it. Continue expanding your systems map until you have achieved an insight, that is, until you have identified a new leverage point that you had not considered before, or you recognize one pivotal issue that, if resolved, would substantially solve your problem. Narrow the scope of your work onto that issue. In our experience, a useful systems map has approximately 5 to 15 boxes.

   Workshop participants working on the Tesla case might take the drivers issue and break it down into access, relative ownership price (how much it costs to own and operate an electric car compared with traditional vehicles), and other buying factors. The logic being that if someone can get access to a new electric car, it makes sense financially to buy it, and if the other buying factors, such as design and performance are met, we should be able to make a sale. Participants would then draw a line connecting technology to relative ownership price. Then, since new technologies can drive down the cost of EVs by, for example, increasing the car's efficiency, the team might shift to building out another primary issue, such as technology.

4. *Decide which key issue(s) to address now.* Finally, you want to select one to three key issues that you think your team should work on immediately. You will not have time to address all of the issues in one day, so you want to focus creative energy on those drivers that will move you most rapidly toward a solution. Write those key issues in the form of questions on the right-hand side. Participants working on the Tesla case might decide in the end to focus on finding a creative way to reduce the erratic fluctuations of oil prices (because when oil prices fall, an electric vehicle becomes a more expensive option) and winning over key partners to establish Tesla as the "must have" technology.

By this point, your team will ideally feel focused and energized. They have explored the problem together, so they have a deeper understanding of its inner workings. They have agreed on a few key issues to work on, and they are excited because they have begun opening up the solution space.

CHAPTER 15

Step 3
Expand

We have more possibilities available in each moment than we realize.

—Thich Nhat Hanh[1]

We think too small, like the frog at the bottom of the well. He thinks the sky is only as big as the top of the well. If he surfaced, he would have an entirely different view.

—Mao Tse-tung[2]

The more options you and your team see, the more likely it is that you will find the silver bullet. Your goal, then, should be to generate more strategic options for addressing your issues than your competition does. In this step, you are seeking to expand the possible solutions that you will consider, ideally generating 50 to 250 ideas. In the next step, described in Chapter 16, you will learn a simple process to rapidly narrow down these possibilities and identify the ones with the greatest disruptive potential.

As we discussed in Chapter 10, what enables some innovative thinkers to see solutions that others overlook is that they overcome a mathematical problem by deploying a mental trick. The math problem is the inherent limitation of humans' capacity for short-term working memory. The trick is using strategic narratives, or patterns, to overcome those limitations and therefore play the game with more moves than their opponents.

Studies of expertise and expert performance give us insight into how they do this. Most people can retain between five and nine items in their short-term working memory. If you go to a grocery store, for example, and have to buy only five things, you may not need a grocery list. But if you have to buy 15 things and do not write a list, you will probably forget something. If you are playing a game that requires that you consider only five options, you can easily think through those options. If you are playing a more complex game, however, one in which you must consider 30 or 100 options, you run out of short-term working memory capacity, and your mind then starts hiding options from you. It simply doesn't have the capacity to show them all.

Experts are able to implement more complex strategies by applying the chunking process we described earlier. It allows them to effectively hold a larger number of ideas in their short-term working memory because they are grouped together into patterns, each of which is composed of multiple pieces.

To enable you and your team to see options that your competition does not see, you also want to play with the larger, more diverse, repertoire of patterns. In this section, we will introduce you to some patterns that may reveal exciting solutions.

The *36 Stratagems*

For the past 10 years, I have been working with a set of strategic narratives found in an ancient Chinese text called the *36 Stratagems* (see Appendix B). I wrote about these stratagems in my first two books: *The Art of the Advantage* and *Hide a Dagger Behind a Smile*. This collection of strategic metaphors was created over the course of 1,000 years, through oral tradition, and written down over a long span of time, between AD 500 and 1500. My research into the competitive dynamics of corporate competition indicates that the stratagems represent a complete vocabulary for describing and managing competition. (See Chapter 20 for more about strategic narratives and how they differ from other types of narratives.)

You will not have time to use all 36 stratagems during your strategizing session—that would take days. Instead, focus on a few that will prove particularly potent. Luckily, we know which those are. The five strategies in the outthinker playbook presented in Part 2 are actually drawn from the 36 stratagems. They are the five stratagems most often used today by companies that are beating their competition.

The following table presents each of the moves in the outthinker playbook next to the original name of the stratagem they come from. Note that these original names were written as much as 1,500 years ago. Their flowery, dramatic language may seem out of place in modern times, but I have attempted to isolate their core lesson. "Smile," for example, was originally "Hide a dagger behind a smile." At first glance, this may seem morally opposite to how we have been interpreting the stratagem, "Be good." But its efficacy rests on the same strategic principle that makes "be good" logical—that by creating a situation in which would-be competitors benefit by your winning, you preempt competition.

What you will do next is use these five stratagems as brainstorming tools to expand your option set. If you want to expand your repertoire even further by exploring more stratagems, see the list in Appendix B.

	Original	**Modern**	**Brainstorming Question**	**Example**
22	Await the exhausted enemy at your ease.	Move early to the next battleground.	Where is the next battleground?	Rosetta Stone in language software
34	Deck the tree with bogus blossoms.	Coordinate the uncoordinated.	Who could you coordinate?	Wikipedia
7	Besiege Wei to rescue Zhao.	Launch a two-front battle.	With whom can you launch a two-front battle?	Virgin Atlantic vs. British Airways
33	Hide a dagger behind a smile.	Be good.	How could you appear to be or truly be helpful?	Vistaprint
32	Create something out of nothing.	Create something out of nothing.	What piece can you add to the board?	Callaway Golf in their addition of new golfers to the game

CASE EXAMPLE: FINANCIAL SERVICES DIVISION

The financing division of a major global PC firm was struggling. Their business depended on systems integrators, the partners who sold servers and other hardware to large companies, feeding them clients who wanted to finance these purchases. But there was no reason for systems integrators to prefer this group's services over those of any other financial service company. Clients were, for the most part, ambivalent about the source of financing as long as the interest rate was competitive; and since this was a highly competitive area, no company could offer meaningfully better rates for any sustained period of time.

Unable to differentiate themselves, this group found their market share and revenue stagnant. How could they start growing revenue? How could they begin winning market share?

The team gathered together seven of their key leaders to brainstorm new, creative strategies for differentiating themselves. They looked at the problem through seven different lenses. By the end of a half-day session, they had generated about 75 possible strategies.

One of the lenses they used is called *exchange a brick for a jade*, which essentially says that you give up something that costs you little in exchange for some form of loyalty or captivity. The team explored what the *brick* could be. What could they give away to systems integrators in exchange for some level of loyalty?

Someone came up with an interesting idea. Since the company had records of the past hardware purchases of many companies in their target region, they could identify which companies were likely going to need to replace their aging hardware soon. This information could be their *brick*.

The team created a new program for systems integrators. Under this program, integrators who guided more clients to this financing division would in return get leads of companies that would soon need to purchase new hardware. By implementing this new strategy, the team differentiated their business and tripled their revenue over the next three years.

The Exercise

Look again at the key strategic issues that you identified in the previous chapter. You are about to begin a brainstorming session, starting with agreeing on the rules you would like to follow as you conduct this session. We suggest agreement on the following ground rules at a minimum.

Ground Rules

- Focus on quantity rather than quality of ideas. Based on our experience, your team should generate between 50 and 250 possible strategies.
- Focus on generating new ideas rather than assessing right now.
- Extract full participation from everyone.
- Write down on Post-it notes every idea generated, regardless of how funny or impossible it may seem.
- Consider some roles. For example, pick one person to be the timekeeper; another person to be the scribe; another to be the crazy one, whose job is to continually throw in seemingly impossible ideas; and someone else to be the agitator, whose job is to jump-start the collective energy whenever things slow down.

Step 1: Adopt a new frame.

Select the first stratagem from your playbook, or any stratagem from the list of 36 in Appendix B. You can also visit my website to access tools to help you apply the right stratagem for the right situation.

Step 2: Write down all ideas that come to mind.

Look at your strategic challenge through the lens of this stratagem, ask the brainstorming questions provided on the previous page (or in the list of the 36 Stratagems in Appendix B), and write down as many ideas as you and your team can come up with. Use Post-it notes or write on a flip chart.

Step 3: Repeat.

Adopt the next stratagem from your playbook, or any stratagem from the list of 36, and repeat steps 1 and 2 until you have looked at your challenge through at least five stratagems.

In a typical session, your team should generate between 50 and 250 potential strategies. If you are producing less than that, something is wrong. Maybe you are not giving yourselves enough permission to really let go and brainstorm. Maybe you are not asking the right strategic question; if so, go back to step 1 described in Chapter 13.

CHAPTER 16

Step 4 Analyze

The world is in a constant conspiracy against the brave. It's the age-old struggle: the roar of the crowd on the one side, and the voice of your conscience on the other.

—Douglas MacArthur[1]

Now that you've created a large number of ideas, your next challenge is to choose which ones you will validate or execute. Your goal is to help your team reach strategic clarity, or define your game plan, and ensure that in doing so you have chosen the most disruptive strategy.

However, be careful not to simply ask yourself, "Which ideas do I like?" If you do, you will in effect be asking yourself, "Which ideas could I see working?" By triggering this visualization process, you are actually asking yourself, "Which ideas have I seen work in some other context?" This usually leads you back to the most obvious or familiar, and all the work you did to come up with so many innovative ideas is for naught.

Another risk that you will face as you sort through the ideas is ending up with creative, rather than disruptive, strategies. Creative ideas are those novel ones that we defined in Chapter 11—customers may love them, but the competition can easily copy them. Disruptive ideas are both novel *and* lead to longer-term competitive advantage because they are the ones that the competition will resist copying. Effective strategic thinkers adopt a disruptive mind-set; they think as much about what the competition will do as they do about what the customer wants—and by following the process outlined here, you can begin developing that same mind-set.

Why did it take HP decades to adopt a version of Dell's *go direct* model? Why did it take American Airlines, Delta, and other traditional airlines 30 years to mount a meaningful counter to Southwest's budget airline model? Great companies fail to adopt great ideas because, initially at least, they fail to recognize an innovative idea as holding strategic value. They are not even willing to invest the time to measure the idea's risks and reward potential.

To help you and your team to overcome these two hurdles—returning to the obvious answers and adopting strategies that are easily copied—we suggest that using a 2 × 2 matrix, you map every idea that you have created. The goals are to find a way to win with the least amount of effort and to find the path of greatest ease.

It is critical that you consider *every* idea. But, since you do not have time to test all of your ideas with rigorous analysis, you must first conduct an initial assessment to decide which are worth the effort. Many great ideas die at this early phase, because, after assessment, the team rules them out.

Believe me, you won't have time to discuss every idea fully. If you start with idea number one, discuss it for 5 minutes, then decide whether to keep it, it will take you an hour to get through 12 ideas. After 3 hours you will have gotten through 36 ideas. By that time you are so tired that the ideas left on the table look pretty good. You think, "We have enough, let's take a break." Your killer idea, your winning move, may be idea number 37. So do a quick assessment of every single idea you have. You want to assess two things: how easy is it to execute this idea, and what is its potential impact?

- *Ease:* Ask yourself, "Is this idea easy to execute? Does it carry low risk? Do we have the capabilities? Can we do it quickly and at a low cost?" Classify the idea as either easy or difficult.
- *Impact:* Ask yourself, "If I had a magic wand and could execute this idea immediately, what would be the payoff, and how long would it take the competition to respond?" It is critical that you ask this second question. If you don't, your strategy is unlikely to be disruptive. Some of the outthinkers I've interviewed ask themselves this question 20 times or more a day. At each meeting, reading each newspaper article, reviewing each new product feature, they are continually asking themselves, "How difficult would it be for the competition to copy this?"

When assessing how long it will take the competition to copy you, it may help to consider the four levels of advantage (I call them the four Cs):

1. *Conceive:* Your competition has not conceived of the idea. How long will it take for them to think of it? Only a minute, once they get word that you are pursuing it. This first level of advantage might give you only a few days. On the other hand, if your idea involves a long research and development cycle and you can keep your work secret, you may be able to give yourself a more lengthy lead time. By the time the competition conceives of the same idea, you will have already completed months of research and development (R&D) work—work they will still have ahead of them.
2. *Consider:* Even after your competition conceives of the idea, they may not consider it worth doing. I imagine that there was a time when someone at HP got word that a small company called Dell was selling PCs directly to consumers. They brought it up at a meeting, and their associates decided that the idea was simply not worth considering because they believed people needed an expert to walk them through the buying process and would therefore buy only from retailers.
3. *Choose:* Your competition may consider the idea—this means having a team research the feasibility and build a business plan—and then

decide not to pursue the idea. I imagine that HP at some point, after Dell had continued growing, put some numbers to paper and looked into whether they should copy Dell's model. Just as a decade earlier, Sears and JC Penney looked into whether they should copy Walmart's model of building stores in suburbs. In the end, the numbers said "no." People don't buy computers directly. People don't drive out to the suburbs to do their shopping. Driving competitors to *choose* not to compete with you is a strong strategy.

4. *Can't:* If your competition waits long enough, you get a chance to build a more permanent competitive advantage. You establish one of the three sources of sustainable advantage—achieve customer captivity, build meaningful economies of scale, or secure preferential access to resources (see full discussion in Chapter 11). Establishing economies of scale requires more strategic creativity than in the past, but it can be done. By the time competitors wake up, it's too late. You have won.

As you assess your ideas, thinking about how the competition will respond, it helps to think about these four levels. You can better calibrate the amount of competitive cushion an idea carries.

Through this process, you will sort all of your ideas into four types of ideas:

1. *Winning moves:* high-impact ideas that are easy to execute. You should probably begin acting on these ideas immediately. They are inexpensive, low risk, and quick to execute, and they can have a major, positive impact on your game.
2. *Tactics:* ideas that are easy to execute but that will not significantly improve your situation. You may want to execute these, but they are not big enough to put on your priority list. You're not going to laminate them on a poster and hang them in the hallways or announce them to market with a press release.
3. *Time wasters:* low impact and difficult to achieve. These ideas are probably wasting resources. We often find that through this exercise companies identify many initiatives that are time wasters. Remove these from your agenda to focus on higher-return efforts.

4. *Crazy:* Ideas that appear difficult to achieve but that could lead to significant strides. These are the "go to the moon" ideas at a time before we had the technology to get to the moon. Most companies kill off these ideas because they are too hard to execute. Innovative companies, by contrast, keep these ideas alive. They do not execute them right now, but they continue to discuss them, looking for ways to improve their achievability. If you don't keep them alive and figure out a way to make them work now, a more creative competitor may figure it out instead.

With this exercise of classifying each idea into these four quadrants, you and your team are forced to consider every idea. You remove completely the common tendency to kill off ideas by refusing to consider them. To complete the process, remove time wasters and tactics from discussion and focus your discussions on how you can turn crazy ideas into winning moves. The magic is in the crazy ideas. These are ideas with true innovative potential.

After mapping every single idea, select two crazy ideas and discuss how you could make them more feasible. This is arguably the most critical step in the process and the one that many other strategy processes miss. It's the crazy ideas that will surprise your competition and drive a real pop in your performance. If you don't allow for time to explore them, you will suffocate your best opportunity for greatness.

One client I was working with, for example, was looking for a way to increase the number of mobile phones that use its software. They had been struggling for years to expand their presence on mobile phones but always came up short. They went through the Outthinker Process and created about 50 ideas, 15 of which they classified as crazy. They picked one of the crazy ideas and brainstormed how they might make it feasible. The exercise revealed a breakthrough: there was one strategic acquisition they could make that would, overnight, turn the tables on their competition. Even after years of looking at the challenge, no one at the company had really considered this idea before or, if they had, had not spent enough time thinking about it to realize it was actually possible.

Spend at least five minutes exploring at least two crazy ideas. You are then ready to choose the three to seven ideas that you are committed to executing or validating. These compose your strategic game plan. After you have established a game plan, over the next few weeks or months, you should validate the ideas on your short list that you are not yet confident that you should execute.

The Exercise

To help you and your team to achieve strategic clarity, follow three steps:

1. Plot each idea on the matrix. For every single idea you generated, ask, "What is the sustainable impact or payoff if we could successfully execute this idea?" and "How easy would it be for us to execute?"
2. Take two crazy ideas and explore how you could make them easier to execute. Move these ideas to the right on the matrix if you are able to find ways to make them more feasible.
3. Define your game plan. Pick three to seven ideas that you and your team are committed to either executing or validating. This is your game plan. You are taking everything else off the table (out of consideration) for now.

CHAPTER 17

Step 5
Sell

Management cannot be expected to recognize a good idea unless it is presented to them by a good salesman.

—David M. Ogilvy[1]

My greatest challenge has been to change the mindset of people. Mindsets play strange tricks on us. We see things the way our minds have instructed our eyes to see.

—Muhammad Yunus[2]

You have devised a brilliant strategic idea. You've asked the right questions, diagnosed the critical issues, conceived a set of unorthodox solutions to address the key issues, narrowed down your ideas into an actionable set of priorities, and now feel confident in your idea. Everything is in line and ready to go.

Sadly, many great ideas fail despite these efforts because the person who presents them cannot sell them effectively to the organization, investors, employees, and so on. You must now think strategically about how you will communicate so that your idea builds support.

To more effectively share your game plan inside your organization, we suggest that you address two issues in the areas of influence:

1. Who do you need to convince?
2. What is your message?

In this chapter we will walk through the steps of building and managing a stakeholder map. The map shows, in black and white, the key individuals and groups who play a role in determining whether your ideas are accepted, and it often reveals valuable insights. It shows whom to influence first, whom to influence later, what indirect influence you should wield, and which stakeholders you should contact. Great influencers seem to do this intuitively. For the rest of us, it helps to sit down with our team and think through our stakeholders with pen and paper in hand. This process will ultimately tell us what our contact strategy should be.

One of my clients, one of the youngest country managers of a leading pharmaceutical company, spends time regularly reviewing his stakeholder map, looking at both internal and external stakeholders. It helps him assess whom he needs to touch base with that week.

Another client, the chief executive officer (CEO) of a publicly traded company, was about to make a major announcement and was concerned with how it would play out in the market. The announcement was overall good news for the company and should propel its stock price upward. But if interpreted incorrectly, the announcement could have spiraled into a negative news story. What made this a potential problem was the company's history with three prominent stock analysts. They had predicted the stock price would fall, and since analysts live and die by the accuracy of their price predictions, they would have a natural motivation to pick up the negative story, rather than the positive one.

To contain this risk, we plotted a stakeholder map. For each player—stock analyst, industry expert, financial journalist, and so on—we assessed how much that person could influence the stock price, what level of influence we had with him or her, and what that person's natural disposition would be (positive, negative, or neutral). We developed a stakeholder management strategy to help ensure that the positive narrative about the announcement would build rapidly, before the negative narrative could take hold.

The results were phenomenal. On the day of the announcement, the stock immediately began to rise. Within a week, it reached its 52-week high, and it went on to continue breaking records. As I finish writing this chapter, in May 2011, I am still getting notices that this stock price is climbing.

Of course, the stock didn't rise simply because of how we managed key stakeholders. The announcement was the result of two years of hard work and investment. The company also produced record quarterly performance. But the stakeholder strategy we implemented worked exactly as we hoped: it preempted a negative narrative from emerging and forced the positive narrative into light.

■ ■ ■

After you have identified whom you need to convince and when, you're ready to plan how you will go about it. You want to think strategically about this as well. I suggest you walk through a four-step process to define your influence. I call this process GAME.

Goal: What do you want to achieve?
Audience: Whom do you need to influence or get input from?
Message: What do you want to say?
Expression: How will you deliver the message?

Goal

Before you launch into your pitch, you need to take the time to really understand whom you are seeking to influence. There are generally three types of outcomes you will want to achieve through your communication; note that "convincing" is not the only one.

1. *To understand:* You may not yet be sure what position someone holds or what role he or she plays view and role.
2. *To loosen:* When someone is in strong opposition and/or when you have multiple opportunities to engage with someone, you may only need to move that person toward being open to another point of view. If you can get him or her to say, "I'm willing to consider alternatives" or "Okay, I'm willing to hear more," that may be all you need to produce agreement.
3. *To convince:* Your goal may be to convince someone of something and have him or her take action on that conviction.

Audience

Having defined the goal, the next step is to understand the person or people you are seeking to influence. To do this effectively, put yourself into their shoes and ask the following questions:

- How aware are they of the issue or idea?
- If they are aware of the issue, how well do they understand it?
- Are they already experts, or do I need to educate them?
- Do they already hold a strong point of view about the issue, and if so, what is that view (positive or negative)?
- Why do they hold that view?

Message

After analyzing the audience, you want to now craft the message that is most likely to achieve your desired outcome. Studies have shown that logic is a relatively ineffective approach to changing minds. Rather, people use nonlogical approaches to make up their minds and only then use logic to support their decision. So you must use something other than logic to convince someone to consider your position and then use logic to lock in the new conviction.

Here are some questions you might ask in deciding how to structure your message.

- How can I open my presentation to engage others? Here's a good framework to consider: situation, complication, question, answer.
- What metaphor do I want to use to frame my idea?
- How can I frame the past facts related to this issue in a way that tells a helpful story—a story that leads people to see that the action I'm suggesting is a natural next step?

Expression

With message in hand, informed by an analysis of your goal and audience, you are now ready to decide how to express your message. Before you jump immediately into planning a presentation, ask some of the following questions:

- Is it better to do this by phone or in person?
- Is it better to circulate a report or give a presentation?
- Should we meet at work or somewhere else?
- If at work, should we meet in the other person's office, my office, or somewhere else (e.g., a site visit)?
- Is it better for us to stand and present with PowerPoint or to sit down and talk in a small group?
- Should we use any props?

Good leaders understand the power of influence; great leaders understand how to focus that influence on the right stakeholder, wrap it in a carefully designed message, and back it up with convincing facts. Take the time now to go through these processes in order to save yourself time and money by following the profitable, and sometimes crazy, ideas.

Our ideas create no value unless we are able to drive their adoption by our colleagues, our organization, and the market. Innovators are, by their nature, effective influencers, able to shape others' points of view. They think strategically not only about what their solution is but also about how they will convince other people of this solution.

The Exercise

1. *Plot key stakeholders on a power-influence matrix.* Complete your stakeholder map by thinking about what key stakeholders will be involved in making the decision of whether to accept or reject your idea. Map all stakeholders on the matrix, thinking about the following:
   a. How much power does each one have over the acceptance of your idea?
   b. How easy it is for you to influence them?
   c. What is their current disposition to your idea?
2. *Develop your contact strategy.* Decide how you will shape the power-disposition matrix (e.g., whom do you want build more influence with and whose power to you want to increase or decrease); then decide which stakeholder you want to approach first.
3. *Define your influence GAME.* Now that you know which stakeholder to approach first, it's time to plan for influencing that occasion. Answer the following questions:
   a. What is my goal? What is my intended outcome, and what do I want this stakeholder to do or believe?
   b. What do I know about my audience (my key stakeholder)?
   c. What message will encourage the audience to do or believe what I want them to do or believe?
   d. How can I engage my audience in my message? Do not automatically turn to a PowerPoint presentation; think more creatively. Can you create a prototype? Can you take them on a site visit?

PART 5

Rebuilding the Organization from Within

As I write this, I am sitting in a hotel lobby in Shanghai, preparing to give a talk to a few hundred General Electric (GE) leaders who represent perhaps 20 different businesses from around the world. While I hope that my talk might spark some ideas that in a few years' time will turn into new growth, GE's challenge, and that of any multinational company of significant size, is bigger.

Helping one business outthink the competition, or helping one leader learn to do this more consistently, is great. But the real opportunity is to achieve these goals across many businesses—across an army of leaders—around the globe. If we can do this, we can truly begin outthinking the competition at every turn, and do this not just today but for decades to come.

This last section is meant to help you realize this larger goal of building a sustainable culture that continually approaches strategic challenges in ways that surprise the market. It is based on work I have done with a number of large multinational companies, some of which I can name and others that I cannot. I believe that the process involves three sequential phases:

1. *Establish multiple points of differentiation.* Calibrate your current level of competitiveness and increase this competitiveness score by introducing new winning moves. This gives you disruptive power today.
2. *Create playbook asymmetry.* Just as great chess players study their opponents' strategic character, you can analyze your competitors' playbooks and thereby predict how they are likely to behave in the future. This allows you to design a unique playbook of your own, one that captures a unique pattern of behavior. Your playbook will ensure that with every strategic move, you further distance yourself from the competition. This helps you sustain your disruptive power as the game evolves.
3. *Construct an outthinker culture.* You embed the playbook you defined in phase 2 into your corporate culture by carefully selecting the strategic narratives that shape your culture. This helps your company avoid the common risk of forgetting your unique playbook and helps build permanent disruptive power.

These three phrases are still a work in process. Establishing a self-sustaining culture of competitiveness takes time, and although the three phases I am suggesting here are showing promising signs of working, we still have a lot to learn as we continue pursuing the dream.

CHAPTER 18

Phase 1 Establish Multiple Points of Differentiation

I am not afraid of an army of lions led by a sheep; I am afraid of an army of sheep led by a lion.

—Alexander the Great[1]

Every year I travel down to Cali, Colombia, to teach a version of my strategy course called *service innovation.* I spend a week with a group of young managers from places like Colgate-Palmolive and Cadbury Schweppes, exploring the anatomy of great service experiences. And every time, someone tells me, "You have *got* to have dinner at Andres Carne de Res." Even friends outside of Colombia—one of my investors from Mexico, my neighbor in Greenwich, Connecticut—passionately promote the restaurant. "It's not like any other restaurant you have experienced," they say. But no one could tell me *why* the experience is so unique. And because my trips to Colombia over the past few years have never coincided with Andres's hours (the restaurant is open only Thursday through Sunday), I always left for home still wondering what all the fuss was about.

But recently, in Colombia delivering a workshop for HP, I finally got my chance to find out. What started out feeling like the Twilight

Zone—we were accosted by a perverted doorman and then three loud maids (read more below)—evolved into the most unique dining experience I have ever known.

How do they do it? I'm going to describe the restaurant's strategy using the same framework I use to teach my service innovation class: the eight Ps.

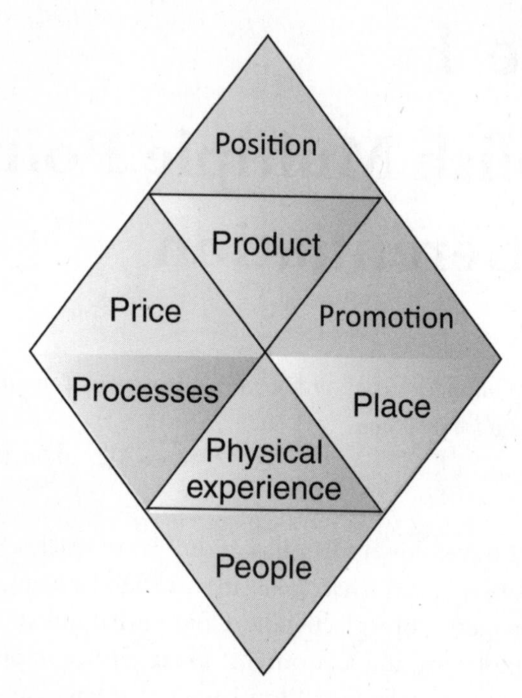

The eight Ps framework says that if you want to create a truly disruptive company, you want to unleash winning moves (strategic choices the competition will not or cannot react intelligently to) across eight dimensions: position, product, price, place, promotion, processes, physical experience, and people. My research shows that you can actually calibrate a company's competitive advantage by using this eight Ps framework to come up with a competitiveness score that correlates with a company's growth rate and profitability. In other words, the more points of differentiation a company can create across the eight Ps and the more sustainable those differences are, the faster the company grows and the more profitable it is.

This makes sense intuitively. Breakthrough companies, companies that have changed their industries, must necessarily differentiate themselves from the competition in a way that customers will love and that competitors will not copy. Dell revolutionized computer retailing by introducing four points of differentiation: product (customized computers), process (assembling computers on demand), place/distribution (directly selling to users), and physical experience (purely phone or online interaction). Walmart grew into the largest retailer in the world by engineering four points of differentiation. Southwest Airlines engineered four points of differentiation to disrupt the traditional airlines. Looking at today's outthinkers, we see Rosetta Stone introducing four points of differentiation; Tesla Motors, five; Genomma Lab, five; and Vistaprint, six.

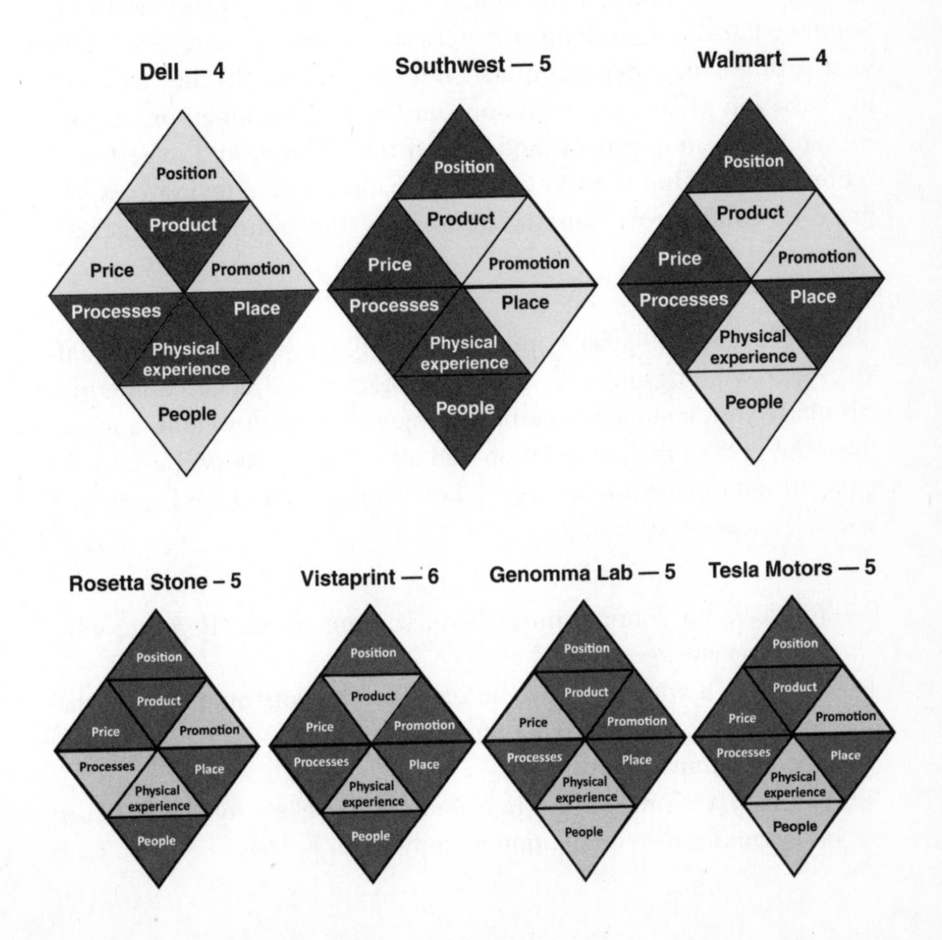

How to Calibrate

Strategy is as much about what you don't do as it is about what you do. A strategy is a set of decisions. If you look at other words that have the same root as *decide*—homicide, suicide, genocide—you see that when you make a decision, you are killing off something—you are making a choice to go along one direction and kill off the path to a different direction. A good strategy is not a this *and* that statement; a good strategy is a this *and not* that statement.

This is important because by making clear decisions, you are choosing a strategy that forces the competition to also kill off something if they want to follow you. You are forcing them to make a choice: copy us and kill off something you value, or just let us be. Southwest Airlines challenged American Airlines to copy the Southwest Airline point-to-point model and kill off the hubs they had built in Dallas and Miami. Rosetta Stone challenges its competitors to copy its natural learning process and kill off their history and expertise in traditional learning theory. Great companies raise copying cost, the price its competitors must incur to copy the outthinker's successful strategy.

The longer it will take your competitor to copy you, the more valuable your winning move is. So, to calibrate the level of competitive advantage you or any other company enjoys, you want to look honestly from the eyes of the competition and ask, "How long will it take the competition to copy my strategy?" Look across each of the Ps and give yourself a score of 0, 1, or 2.

0—You have no winning move here; you are essentially doing what everyone else does.

1—You have a winning move and are doing something unique that matters to consumers, but a motivated competitor would be able to copy it within four years.

2—You have a winning move in place, and it is likely to take five years or longer for the competition to copy you.

Competitiveness Calibration

	0—no winning move	1—competition can copy within four years	2—competition will take five years or longer to copy	Total score
Position				
Product				
Price				
Place/ distribution				
Promotion				
Processes				
Physical experience				
People				
			Total score:	______

Sun Tzu says that you want to leave multiple traps; this way, if your adversaries do not step into one trap, they back into another. You want to lay many traps for your competition, force them into a number of dilemmas, and give them as many reasons as you can to *not* copy you. This will create space for your business to grow uncontested.

You can use the Outthinker Process to generate multiple winning moves for each of the eight Ps.

Examples of Winning Moves across the 8Ps

Position	The key to creating a positioning advantage is to differentiate yourself in your customers' minds in at least two dimensions and hold positions in those dimensions that your competition will not want to occupy. Urban Outfitters, a fast-growing U.S. clothing retailer, markets only college-age students. Traditional competitors, like Gap, will resist copying this positioning because

(*continued*)

(continued)

	to do so would be to give up other important market segments, like baby, maternity, and, generally, adults. Urban Outfitters also differentiates itself by making every store look a little different. Gap, who depends on efficiencies gained by every store looking similar, will resist adopting Urban Outfitters's layout strategy. Of course, traditional competitors can replicate this "college student–focused and every store unique" positioning with a new brand, a new concept, or a new area in each store, but that takes years of planning. While competitors plan, Urban Outfitters grows.
Product	Nintendo introduces the Wii, a game console with a motion-sensor device that allows players to manipulate video games with natural movements. With this innovation, this relatively small player lurched ahead of larger competitors Microsoft and Sony, who took years to respond with competing products.
Price	Creating a winning move in pricing is rarely about offering a lower price; it involves pricing differently. Redbox, for example, places vending machines in supermarkets where customers can rent DVD movies. The concept was originally developed by McDonald's and was then spun off as an independent business. Redbox prices its DVDs at $1 per day, whereas traditional competitors price their rentals (online or physical) at $3 to $4 per rental. By pricing per day, Redbox creates the perception that customers can rent a video for one-third the price. But because customers rarely return their video in one day, they often end up paying much more than they would have had they rented from the competition. By changing the basis of pricing, Redbox charges more but creates the perception that it charges less.
Place/ distribution	Dell revolutionizes computer selling by selling directly to consumers; Rosetta Stone challenges industry norms by selling through kiosks rather than bookstores; Salesforce.com is one of the first to offer "software as a service," delivering software through a web interface rather than having customers spend millions to install software on their own servers.
Promotion	Vistaprint spends little or no money on traditional promotion. Instead, it offers customers free business cards (customers pay only for shipping). The business cards have the customer's design on the front and a small Vistaprint logo on the back. This strategy

	lowers barriers to trying the Vistaprint service, encourages peer-to-peer marketing (when customers hand out business cards, they are spreading the Vistaprint brand), and lowers marketing costs (the marginal cost to print new cards is minimal). By not having to spend on traditional advertising, Vistaprint is able to achieve gross margins above 50 percent.
Processes	Corporate Creations helps companies register their businesses across multiple jurisdictions. It is rapidly challenging an oligopoly controlled by two entrenched competitors. One strategy is its unique employee compensation process. It starts by running an open book, so all employees know every month exactly what the company's revenue and profit was. It then gives monthly bonuses based on that month's gross profit. This forces employees to be accountable to each other and work as a team. Vistaprint forces customers to use the same size and paper type, then consolidates customer orders into one large batch. This lets them produce small orders of business cards at a fraction of the cost of its competitors.
Physical experience	When Apple launched Apple Stores, many viewed this as a dangerous diversion from the core. But the stores have achieved one of the highest revenue per square foot of retailers around the world, and they allow Apple to better manage the physical experience customers have with the Apple brand. When you buy a Dell or HP computer, you interact with the brand remotely (via phone or Internet) or indirectly (through a retailer's salesperson). With Apple, you can, usually with a short drive, directly interact with an Apple expert in an Apple environment.
People	Rosetta Stone does not hire traditional learning experts; instead, it hires people who have learned a second language naturally. Vistaprint does not hire printing experts; it hires young, technology-savvy marketers. Urban Outfitters does not hire retailing experts; it hires "sensory merchandisers" that it can trust to make decisions about how to decorate their individual stores.

The magic really comes into play when the winning moves you have introduced across the eight Ps cross-fertilize each other. Urban Outfitters's people decision—hiring sensory merchandisers—creates a process winning move: local managers' job descriptions allow them to change their store's look and feel. This, in turn, creates a physical experience winning move: every store looks different. By linking winning moves, you raise the copy cost your competitors must consider.

Andres Carne de Res is the first company I have ever come across that introduces winning moves across all eight Ps. They could, if they chose, leverage their competitive strength into becoming a worldwide restaurant chain, but they won't. This is not the company's vision.

1. *Product:* Let's start with the basics. Andres Carne de Res offers a long menu of creative dishes. We started with chunks of pork (chicharrones) served on a long, flat, wooden bowl with a side of cilantro guacamole dipping sauce. Local beers are served with a paper yellow butterfly pasted to their bottle necks. Wine is served in bottles individually hand-painted in bright colors by local artists.
2. *Price:* The price refers not just to actual prices, but also to how they are communicated and how customers pay. When we asked for the menu, our server gave us a metal case about the size of shirt box. Inside was a scroll, and when you crank a handle at the bottom or top, a menu rolls up or down. It felt like an ancient Egyptian website that you scrolled down to see offerings and prices.
3. *Place:* Andres Carne de Res is nearly 30 years old. It is packed every night it's open, and people talk about it from all over the world. But the restaurant has only two locations. One is in a distant suburb, a farm really, 30 minutes outside of Bogota. Two years ago they opened their second location: a four-story maze in one of Bogota's chicest shopping districts. I went to this newer location to avoid a long trip.
4. *Promotion:* As far as I can tell, Andres runs no promotions. They rely exclusively on word of mouth. Rather than advertise in newspapers, as most restaurants do, they provide unique artifacts—like hand-painted wine bottles and a coffee table book—that make it easy for people to share their *Andres experience* with their friends. That's what got me there, and judging from the packed tables and dance floors, the no-promotion strategy is serving Andres just fine.
5. *Position:* It's hard to fit Andres into a box. It felt somewhat like an original Hard Rock Café, a quirky space filled with interesting pieces of art and paraphernalia. But it is far more than a theme restaurant. It has three dance floors, a stage, a piano, and a DJ, and actors interrupt

your meal every now and then, playing funny improv scenes, which make you think of a funky Disney resort.

6. *Processes:* Behind the scenes this multisensory experience is supported by an uncommon orchestration. I could not figure out how they engineered it, but we must have been helped over the evening by at least seven different people who passed us off as seamlessly as the Brazilian World Cup team passes around a ball. In college, I spent three years waiting tables and came to understand that the best way to guarantee a seamless experience is to dedicate one server to each table. Andres proves this dogma wrong.
7. *People:* When we walked through the restaurant's door I was a bit surprised by the characters hanging out trying to get in. One, wearing a bandana, thin mustache, and a suit that looked something like a security guard's uniform, was offering in a loud voice to pat down women visitors for weapons. At the stair landing, three women dressed as maids commented loudly that whoever had ironed my shirt had done a terrible job and offered to take care of it for me. About one-third of Andres' 1,000 or so employees seem to be actors. Their job is simply to play interesting characters and entertain the guests all night.
8. *Physical experience:* Finally, Andres has created a physical experience that I truly cannot describe. I lack the skill to do it justice with my words. There were fresh-cut roses hanging on strings above our heads, butterfly-shaped confetti fell from the sky, industrial metal staircases led you from hell up to purgatory then to heaven. A huge fireplace sat on a landing between hell and purgatory and a 10-foot-tall bust of Jesus hung from heaven's floor (ceiling?). As the DJ's music seduced the diners to abandon tables for dance floors, the restaurant evolved, revealing layers and layers of intricate surprises.

The case of Andres Carne de Res suggests that you consider at least two things. First, of course, get yourself to Bogota and experience it for yourself. Second, look for what you can do across all eight dimensions to design a truly unparalleled, disruptive customer experience. Consider applying the Outthinker Process to answer these questions:

- What can we do with our product that competitors will not copy?
- How can we more creatively establish and communicate prices, and collect payment?

- How can we promote more innovation?
- How can we challenge the accepted distribution model (place)?
- What competitive position relative to competitors can we command that competitors will not want to copy?
- What processes innovation can we introduce that would create a competitive advantage?
- How can we change how we hire and inspire our people?
- How can we make the physical experience of our product or service unique?

Working through these questions is not an overnight or one-day job. It is a journey, one that may never end. But if you pick up one of these challenges each quarter, you will be stretching ahead of your competitors more quickly than they will be able to catch up.

CHAPTER 19

Phase 2 Create Playbook Asymmetry

You win battles by knowing the enemy's timing, and using a timing which the enemy does not expect.

—Miyamoto Musashi[1]

All history teaches that no enemy is so insignificant as to be despised and neglected by any power, however formidable.

—Antoine-Henri Jomini, *Art of War*[2]

The points of differentiation you created through Chapter 18 will, if well designed, protect you from competitive pressure for years. But they still have a shelf life. Eventually your continued success will create too strong a pull for imitators to resist. It took several decades, but HP eventually embraced Dell's *go direct* model. Traditional software companies eventually answered the challenge Salesforce.com made when it rallied behind the slogan "death to software" and promoted software as a service, or cloud computing.

Or perhaps you must change your carefully designed strategy (your eight Ps) for other reasons. Maybe new opportunities emerge or market dynamics shift suddenly. Whatever the cause, your first thought must be, How will our people react? Will they respond predictably, in lock-step with the competition, or will their responses propel us yet further ahead of the pack?

So to lengthen the longevity of your strategic advantage, you must think carefully about how you want your organization to behave. Think of it this way. Genghis Khan's Mongol army did not win because they planned each battle more carefully than their opponents. Indeed, they probably planned less. They won because they had adopted a natural set of behaviors that was different from the competition. That set of behaviors is what I am calling a playbook, and the difference made it asymmetrical to the opponents.

Traditional competitive intelligence helps you plan today's battle, but not the series of battles that compose the war. It helps you understand what the competition is likely to do this year, but not how they are likely to react to future new opportunities. To win for the long term you need something more.

U.S. businesses have a long tradition of studying customer behavior. We use focus groups, interviews, and surveys; we hire marketing firms, anthropologists, and innovation consulting firms to gather customer insight. Understanding customer behavior is surely valuable, but competitive behavior matters just as much.

One of my clients, eager to develop a three-year competitive strategy, had spent hundreds of thousands of dollars gathering customer research, identifying high-potential market opportunities, and analyzing the competition in each one. At the end of the long and expensive process, the company had exactly what it wanted: a three-year strategy. But then executives realized that in three years, the markets would have evolved and formerly strong opportunities would have become overcrowded.

They needed something with a longer shelf life, and that's where we came in. We helped them develop a playbook. First, we analyzed the playbooks of two key competitors, studying past behaviors, unique organizational structures, and other factors. We then helped the client develop its own playbook, not one that copied the competition but that intelligently contrasted with them. We created playbook asymmetry.

For reasons of confidentiality I cannot provide details, but to give you a sense of what real playbook asymmetry looks like, here are some of the elements, in disguise, that we have helped clients develop.

Competitive Behavior	**Our Opportunity**
One of the competitors has divided its organization by men's and women's brands. This means it would be relatively difficult for it to pursue unisex brands.	Our client saw that if it pushed forward with a unisex brand in any market segment, the competition would be slow to respond.
One competitor is heavily focused on scale; it has a tradition of developing products locally and then turning them into global brands. The company shies away from products with purely local appeal.	Our client increased its investment in local-only products, knowing the competition had natural disposition away from doing something similar.
One competitor has a habit of being second to market, letting other innovators build the market first.	Our client decided to aim to be either first or third: developing or acquiring cutting-edge technologies before others commercialized them or letting the competitor take second place while preparing to follow closely behind.
One competitor manages its many brands in a coordinated fashion, making sure its brand attributes and target customers do not overlap.	Our client took a less controlled approach, giving brand managers more rein to compete with each other, thereby blocking out the competition from the edges.

I could go on with examples, but I think these make the point. Your competitors are going to follow a pattern of behavior, either out of habit or for more structural reasons. By stopping to assess their behaviors (their playbook), you can make a more intelligent choice about what behaviors to adopt to make your playbook asymmetrical. In the next chapter we will talk about how to embed these behaviors into your organizational culture.

Understanding Playbooks—Theirs and Yours

Developing your competitors' playbooks and then your own takes time and effort but is not especially difficult. We have found it efficient to follow a seven-step process.

Step 1. Pick Your Top Competitors

From the age of one year, my eldest son's favorite band has been what he calls *Me Too*, known to the rest of us as U2. In one of his songs, the lead singer Bono sings, "Choose your enemies carefully 'cause they will define you." Choose one to three competitors that you want to create playbook asymmetry with. Be careful whom you pick because that choice could have a profound influence on the strategy you ultimately adopt.

Pick competitors that serve the customers you want to serve, offer the types of products and services you want to excel at offering, and are in the types of businesses you can define as your sandbox. One of our clients, for example, chose two seemingly unrelated competitors—a global beauty company and a consumer products leader—as comparisons because they viewed themselves as playing in the intersection of these two businesses.

You will not be copying your competitors' strategy. A *me too* strategy can never give you a significant lead; instead, you will create yours as a contrast, as a mirror. Think about what industries you compete in and pick one of the most significant, prototypical players in that industry.

Step 2. Pick Your Lenses

I was conducting a workshop for a client, and the company's head of strategy was one of the participants. He said that when he had joined the company a year earlier, he thought he knew it well because he had already been a client for 10 years. But once he switched from client to employee, he realized he had looked through only one window of a huge house. There was so much more to learn.

You need to pick a few critical lenses from which to analyze your competitor. The bigger the team you have working on this, the more lenses you can pick. Consider the following:

- Organization structure
- Recruitment
- Talent development
- Culture
- Financial structure
- Investor base
- Research and development (R&D) processes
- New product launch processes
- Marketing
- Pricing strategy
- Geographic reach
- Sales
- Merger and acquisition history
- Strategic partnerships
- Logistics and sourcing
- Operations management
- Related companies (e.g., affiliates)

Step 3. Organize Your Team

After you have picked the lenses with which to look at your competition, you need to decide who is going to gather the information for each lens. For example, if you picked organizational structure and recruitment, you want to assign one team to gather organizational charts, bios of top management, and other organizational information and have another team study the competitor's job board, recent hires, and other recruiting information.

Step 4. Gather Data

Think expansively about what kind of data you can draw from. The more creative you are, the less expensive the data will be and the more likely you are to find something new and useful. Consider all of these sources:

- Your employees who once worked for the competitor
- Your salespeople who have competed with the competitor
- Annual reports and securities filings
- Stock analyst reports
- Advertising (e.g., billboards, TV commercials)
- Newspaper and magazine articles
- Industry trade journals
- Sales materials (e.g., brochures)
- Industry databases
- Industry reports
- Company directories (e.g., Dun & Bradstreet)
- Company histories (e.g., the *Encyclopedia of Company Histories*)
- Trade associations
- Direct observation (e.g., during competitive sales situations)
- Your personal network

Step 5. Consolidate the Data into Key Insights

Now you probably have much more data than you need. When this happens, it becomes difficult to isolate insights. Have your team consolidate the data into groupings and prepare a key insight for each grouping. For example, they may consolidate data about the competitor's organizational structure onto 30 PowerPoint slides and then group those slides into three different bundles. Once they step back and look at the bundles, they should be able to summarize them as a key insight.

This is not just an executive summary in smaller font. It requires you and your team to ask, "So what?" and then arrive at a conclusion that suggests how the competitor may behave. You wouldn't, for example, simply compile all of the competitor's job board listings; rather, you would summarize them as, "They are hiring heavily for marketing people in India" or "They are looking for new Java programmers."

Step 6. Create Their Playbook

After your entire team has had a chance to absorb the key insights—a process that could require several meetings to share and discuss findings—you should be ready to define what you think the competitors' playbook is. The *36 Stratagems* (see Appendix B) is a great framework for doing this. Your goal is to create a complete, concise list of behaviors that you expect your competitor will repeat. Here's an example from one of our clients—disguised, of course.

ABC Competitor's Playbook

1. Exchange a brick for a jade: They will lose money on new products today to make money tomorrow.
2. Take the unorthodox path: They will look for an alternative route to the customer.
3. Exchange the role of guest for that of host: They will take a weaker position with clients and partners and then build power.
4. Beat the grass to startle the snake: They will launch small attacks (releasing betas) to test market reaction before really committing.
5. Coordinate the uncoordinated: They will seek to coordinate other players (customers, vendors, legislators) to build power.

Step 7. Define Your Own Playbook

You now have quite a massive amount of data synthesized into a simple playbook that your competitors use. At this point you are ready to design your own. Following the same steps you just completed for your competition, look now at your own company—your historical behavior, the plays that have generated the most value for you, the ways your culture is unique—and write down a few plays that you think are already part of your competitive character.

Then compare your playbook with your competitor's and decide how you think yours should change. It's very tempting to simply copy your competition. "They are exchanging bricks for jades, so we should, too!" But copying your competitor's playbook is precisely what you should avoid, for it erases any playbook asymmetry you might otherwise develop.

It helps to play a war game exercise. Start by picking a hypothetical opportunity (e.g., launching a new product targeted at men of a particular age). Have half of your team play the competitor and develop the best strategy they can, while the other team plays your company and does the same. Then share what your relative strategies will be. Discuss who is likely to win and how your playbook might need to change to make sure the winner is you.

Conclusion

You may not want to think so, but whatever advantage you have today has a shelf life. To sustain your lead, you must develop a unique set of strategic behaviors—a playbook—that will differentiate you from your competition on an ongoing basis. To do this, analyze the competitors' playbook and develop an intelligent asymmetrical playbook of your own. This typically requires seven steps.

CHAPTER 20

Phase 3 Construct an Outthinker Culture

Vary your methods. This will confuse people, especially your rivals, and awaken their curiosity and attention. If you always act on your first intention, others will foresee it and thwart it. It is easy to kill the bird that flies in a straight line, but not one that changes its line of flight. . . . The consummate player never moves the piece his opponent expects him to, and, less still, the piece he wants him to move.

—Balthasar Gracian, *The Art of Worldly Wisdom*, Chapter 17[1]

History is the version of past events that people have decided to agree upon.

—Napoleon Bonaparte[2]

At the close of 2004, as most of the Western world was celebrating the year-end holidays, unwrapping gifts, lighting candles, and sitting down to family dinners, Indonesians were bracing for catastrophe. Those who could, evacuated on planes. Most simply watched the ocean anxiously, looking for tsunami waves to rise on the horizon.

On December 26, 2004, a magnitude 9.0 earthquake, the largest recorded in 40 years, erupted under the Indian Ocean, triggering waves that towered as high as 12 feet when they hit land. The catastrophe killed 230,000 people, including 9,000 visiting tourists; destroyed entire villages; and displaced millions.

Although most victims had no way of anticipating the waves or, if they could, did not know what to do, the people in the Indonesian town of Simeulue behaved quite differently. Interviews of survivors on that island described a common story:

- They felt an earthquake.
- They saw the ocean water was receding.
- They recognized these as a sign that a wave was coming.
- They ran for high ground.

At a time when most Indonesians were at a loss for how to respond to emerging unrecognizable conditions, the people of Simeulue had an advantage. A tool to quickly assess the situation and adopt a strategy that might save their lives was available to them in the form of a story—the story of the tsunami of 1907.

Passed down through generations, this story had morphed into folklore among the Simeulue people. It took on several distinct variations, but each reinforced the proper response to a common sequence of events. The essence of the story, its moral, is this: if you feel an earthquake and you see the water has receded, do not run to the water to take the fish left there, for they are poisonous; instead, run for the hilltop because a wave will come.

So when the people of Simeulue recognized the first elements of this story's plot had been realized, they immediately, unthinkingly played out the rest. They ran for the hills. The story, told and retold through the years, saved lives.[3]

This is the profound value of narratives. Much of human behavior—94 percent, scientists say—is determined by subconscious thought, and much of that is determined by stories we use to navigate daily challenges. How your people choose to act depends on which stories they tell themselves.

Stories, when used strategically, are vital, practical leadership tools. Those who seek to shape the culture of large organizations use multiple tools: values, missions, scorecards, performance reviews, reporting structures, and dashboards, among others. Effective leaders also embrace a more elusive implement: the strategic narrative. They apply these narratives consciously and strategically, as a way to build a unique culture and a competitive advantage. Overlook them and you are leaving a powerful leadership tool unutilized.

Common Misconceptions about Narratives

Many leaders overlook, or even resist, the power of strategic narratives because stories and storytelling carry unhelpful misconceptions. Narratives are often erroneously considered to be nice to have and confused with organizational values. "We already have defined our corporate values, why do we need to now define our narratives?" they ask.

Narratives Are Nice to Have

When I talk to people about strategic narratives, many at first think I am talking about the softer, "nicer" art of storytelling. They see stories as flourishes, a way to wrap messages in emotion. The common view is that some people are naturally skilled at this art, but for the rest of us, we can compensate by applying more hard-nosed tools, like scorecards and lists of strategic priorities.

But strategic narratives are more than optional flourishes. They are practical and necessary tools for influencing strategy. Some of the toughest, most practical-minded, hard-nosed leaders are strong believers in the power of narrative. John Rogers, Goldman Sachs' long-time chief of staff, is known by colleagues we spoke to as a practical and results-driven leader who exerts enormous power within the firm and beyond. He is also known as the firm's *culture czar*, and he believes passionately in the importance of storytelling. Roger Penske, founder of the Penske Corporation, is another hard-nosed leader who uses narratives strategically, not as artistic flourishes, but as practical tools for producing results.

The importance of strategic narratives is emerging across numerous domains. A growing number of military theorists, for example, are exploring more deeply the role they play in determining the outcome of conflicts.[4] Studies show that the types of stories entrepreneurs tell affect their ability to attract capital.[5] Narratives are powerful tools for winning support and changing minds.[6] They have proved to play practical roles in medicine, cognitive science, sports, chess, and, of course, leadership.[7]

To discount storytelling as a "nice to have" is a mistake. All leaders should look at how the stories they are telling influence strategy, behaviors, and performance.

Narratives and Values Are Interchangeable

The story of the Simeulue illustrates another important point. Many people use the terms *narratives* and *values* interchangeably. On the surface, this seems reasonable, since leaders seem to use both to achieve similar goals: to underscore priorities or encourage a desired behavior. But cultures and organizations with similar values can adopt radically different behaviors.[8] People in well-off communities and those in poorer ones share desires for financial security and family, but the strategies they know to pursue them often look radically different.[9] I have studied corporate rivalries with clear winners and losers and have found that often they share the same values. This is usually because the winner adopts a superior set of values and the loser starts shifting its values to copy the winner.

CarMax, for example, starts beating its larger rival AutoNation in the used car retail business and then AutoNation actually changes its values to be more like CarMax. Motorola did the same with Nokia in the past decade when Nokia took Motorola's lead. If you start winning, your competition will start copying your values. This is why strategic narratives become so important.

Strategic narratives operate separately from values, maybe even more directly. And they can help prevent organizations from growing rigid. Organizations with strong cultures, with deeply rooted core beliefs and values, often grow rigid because they stop learning.[10] In that situation, strategic narratives can serve as a work-around of sorts, allowing leaders to introduce new behaviors without going through the painstaking process of trying to change a company's value system.

I saw this many times in my research. By showing people a new way to achieve a value they already hold, effective leaders can often trigger an immediate, noticeable shift in behavior. Changing narratives is a way to more quickly change culture.

Strategic Narratives

Most of what is written about narratives falls into two categories: deep narratives and planning narratives. Deep narratives are stories about the company or the leader, stories that describe how we got here and where we're going, and they ultimately create meaning. These types of stories are important. They enable leaders to create meaning for others and effectively link their individual stories to deeply rooted organizational stories.[11] But we found few leaders use narratives in this way, outside of formal leadership programs.

Planning narratives are those stories that illuminate a company's strategic plan. A leader using a planning narrative finds a way to conceptualize the strategic plan as a story in order to facilitate understanding and build buy-in.[12] 3M, for example, has successfully rethought its strategic planning process as a process of building stories.[13]

But the most effective leaders, when they use narratives, usually turn to a different kind of story, a third category we call *strategic narratives*. Strategic narratives are different. They are short, memorable, sticky stories that tell people how to behave. When the water recedes, run (the Simeulue). When you must choose between getting eyeballs or selling ads, get eyeballs . . . the money will come (Google).

Strategic narratives differ from deep and planning narratives in at least three ways: their plot is far shorter, they are told to influence behavior (not create identity or sell a vision), and they are intended to have an immediate impact.

One of the best comes from Carlo (which is not his name), a top executive at a company whose name is known around the world. He is the featured actor in a story that others in the organization love to tell. We call it *The Notebook*.

Carlo runs the company's sales and marketing division, some 40,000 people, and spends a substantial amount of time on the road, visiting customers with his account managers.

One day he and a certain account manager called on a customer's chief information officer. The conversation started off informally but soon dove into an involved discussion about the customer's needs and experiences. Carlo was rapidly writing notes on one of the legal pads he always carries with him, capturing everything he thought important.

Suddenly he felt a light tap on his shoulder. The account manager turned toward Carlo and quietly asked, "Do you have a piece of paper I can borrow?" Carlo leaned in as if to whisper; the account manager leaned in to hear. Carlo paused, looked the account manager straight in the eye, and said, "No."

With the right dramatic pause, a story like this becomes sticky and spreads broadly. People who hear it laugh and want to tell it again. The teller and listener may share the story for the humor, but they are also simultaneously propagating an important set of messages about listening to customers and demonstrating that we value what they say. Oh, and being prepared with your own pen and paper.

This is an example of a strategic narrative. They are short, memorable, "sticky" stories that tell people how to behave.

	Deep Narratives	**Planning Narratives**	**Strategic Narratives**
Plot duration	20–100 years (the lifetime of the company or leader)	3–10 years (recent company history plus a 3- to 5-year planning horizon)	A moment to a few hours

	Deep Narratives	Planning Narratives	Strategic Narratives
Purpose	To build identity and purpose	To sell a vision and/or strategy	To promote a behavior
Duration of intended impact	10 years to a lifetime	3–5 years	The moment

Warren Buffett is a brilliant spinner of strategic narratives. For example, to make the point that he does not believe in paying bankers for advice, he uses a recognizable metaphor: "Never ask a barber if he thinks you need a haircut."[14] He then goes on to tell the story of First Boston, which in the 1980s was searching for a buyer for Scott Fetzer, a collection of small businesses. First Boston called 30 firms to drum up interest, with no success. Later, when Buffett decided to call Scott Fetzer's chief executive officer (CEO) personally and directly negotiate a deal to acquire the company, First Boston claimed they were still entitled to a $2 million fee. A First Boston banker asked Buffett's partner, Charlie Munger, if he'd like to read First Boston's report on the company. Munger responded, "I'll pay $2 million *not* to read it."

These are the kinds of stories effective leaders tell. These are strategic narratives.

Strategic narratives help people shift priorities by giving them mental space to absorb a new message.[15] Richard Lyons, former chief learning officer at Goldman Sachs and now dean of the Haas School of Business at Berkeley, put it this way. "If you say 'diversity and inclusion' people hear you briefly. But if you then tell a real story about 'diversity and inclusion' you give people time to process what this really means."[16]

■ ■ ■

Think carefully about the strategic narratives you tell, for they can have a profound impact on your company's culture. Consider the case of Sue, a disgruntled Time Warner Cable customer.

Sometime in 2009 a picture of Kathleen Cattrall, Vice President of Branded Customer Experience at Time Warner Cable, appeared in

USA Today. "It was a really big picture," she says. "It had my name and title, which has the word 'customer' in its title, and the company name. So I started getting all kinds of phone calls from customers and tried to call all of them back."[17]

Kathleen got one call from a customer named Sue. When Kathleen returned the call, she learned a disturbing story. Sue was a Time Warner Cable Internet customer who had learned of a better deal that Time Warner Cable was offering. She asked for a refund for what she perceived as overcharges during the time she was paying a higher rate. She made a series of calls to Time Warner Cable's Customer Service but never got a resolution. Worse, she felt she was treated poorly throughout. So she switched to a competitor.

Kathleen was not able to convince Sue to come back to Time Warner Cable, but she was able to give her something more valuable—a sense that she was heard and appreciated.

When Kathleen later got a card from Sue recounting her experience and suggesting Kathleen share her story as a lesson on how not to treat customers, Kathleen jumped at the opportunity. First, she started carrying around Sue's card. At meetings she would pull it out, read it and tell the story of Sue, making the point that Time Warner Cable needed to build customer-centricity into its DNA.

The story of Sue proved so effective that Kathleen decided to elevate it further. Her group was developing a leadership program for 400 field leaders around the country. They decided that Sue had to be at each one of those trainings, so they produced a life-sized picture of her and incorporated her into the program, all with Sue's approval, of course. Kathleen took these road shows across the country to educate senior leaders on how their decisions affect the customer experience.

The result is that now in meetings and workshops, people don't talk about nameless customers; they talk about "Sue." By personifying the problem, Kathleen and her team found people related more quickly and cared more passionately about making sure all the Sues would feel appreciated and satisfied. The campaign to improve customer satisfaction and commitment has produced measurable results: the portion of highly committed customers has grown across all of Time Warner Cable's regions, improving nearly 10 percent in the past year.[18]

The story of Sue lives on. Recently a Time Warner Cable employee named Adam was checking in at the Cleveland airport. The agent had skipped lunch to help her colleagues, who were busy handling long passenger lines. Her lunch box was sitting just behind the counter, labeled with her name. Adam looked at the box, then at the agent's name badge, then at the agent, and asked, "Are you *the* Sue?" And the agent, who must have heard the question many times before, replied, "Do you work for Time Warner Cable?"

Strategic narratives are important tools for shifting priorities and shaping your company's collective behavior because they begin taking effect immediately and they help keep alive—in working memory—the priority that leaders want people to focus on. In a faster-paced, more competitive world, where the ability to adapt quickly is paramount, strategic narratives can play a critical role. And they are more permanent, because as the stories you tell are told and retold, they weave themselves into the fabric of your culture and become permanent fixtures.

Making It Happen

Strategic narratives can have a meaningful and profound impact on your organization in three ways: they can help you rapidly shift your company's strategic priorities, they can help your people see more innovative solutions to business problems, and they can help establish a set of behaviors (a playbook) that directly impact your company's real strategy. It can take years, but I have seen firsthand how profound the impact can be. After working through the process a few times, I have found these four steps a useful way to proceed:

1. Observe.
2. Collect.
3. Refine.
4. Syndicate.

	1. Observe	2. Collect	3. Refine	4. Syndicate
Description	Determine the current state of your organization through detailed observation of prevailing behaviors and stories. Notice where things are not aligned with the playbook you want your company to adopt (see Chapter 19 for instructions on how to determine your desired playbook).	Look for stories in your own personal history, in your organization's history, and from around your organization that you can use to exemplify and underscore desired traits or behaviors.	Craft these stories into compelling, "sticky" narratives. Practice them in large and small audiences, notice how people respond, and refine them to improve their effectiveness.	Build a repertoire of narratives and share them through multiple channels; notice how effectively they are propagating on their own.
Questions to ask	What behaviors are people repeating? What stories are they currently telling? What do their word choices tell you about how they see things? What behaviors match your	What are the most memorable moments in your personal life? What moments do you most remember from your professional life? What stories from inside your	How can you give the narrative a surprising opening? (Eric Lange, Nielsen's head of human resources, opens one of his favorite strategic narratives with a dramatic depiction of a walk he took with Roger Penske.) What part of the narrative will make it "sticky"? What will	With what system can you keep your repertoire on the "tip of your tongue?" (One CEO of a Fortune 500 company keeps a matrix of narratives and jokes cross-referenced by audience type, geography, and industry sector

(*continued*)

	1. Observe	2. Collect	3. Refine	4. Syndicate
Questions to ask (*continued*)	desired playbook or can give you a competitive advantage? What existing behaviors do you want to remove? What behaviors do you want to add/reinforce?	organization catch your attention? How can you use each of these stories to emphasize the behaviors you want to introduce or reinforce?	make people enjoy retelling it? (James P. Gorman, CEO of Morgan Stanley, tells stories about himself doing things you wouldn't expect from a CEO; this humor makes the retelling pleasurable.) What sensory anchor can you give the narrative so that people can recall it quickly? (A leader at Levi's in South Korea called her turn-around initiative *soom korughi*, a Korean term meaning the breath you take just before exerting great effort.) Do people pay attention when you tell the narrative? How can you play with your rhythm and tone to increase effectiveness? Have you heard people repeating the narrative? (Bob McCann, an executive vice president at Nielsen, thinks about techniques such as "repeating in threes" to maximize the impact of his message.)	to enable rapid recall.) Can you launch a formal program to engage large groups of people in the narratives (such as a top-talent learning program or a formal collection of company stories)? Can you link your narratives to an existing company value statement (e.g., by showing people this new behavior is a way to achieve a value they already hold as important)? What periodic meetings can you leverage to share your narratives? (Kevin Turner at Microsoft holds regular "wire-side chats" and staff meetings.)

Conclusion

In the previous chapter you defined your company's unique, disruptive playbook. Your final challenge is to embed this playbook into your culture so that it becomes second nature—so that, like the Simeulue, your people adopt a unique, coordinated set of behaviors that they employ subconsciously. The way to do this is through strategic narratives—storytelling.

Storytelling is not an optional skill. It is a necessary tool that all leaders would do well to master. It is the means by which you can gradually guide your team into new territory.

Shifting behavior, aligning it with your desired playbook, takes time. But you will begin seeing evidence of new behavior fairly soon. New ideas will flow. Disruptive competitive moves will be noticed by the market and investors. You have set your company on a path to an outthinker culture that may last for generations.

APPENDIX A

The Research

Earlier in this book, I mentioned how much I enjoy listening to the stories business leaders tell. The stories in themselves are captivating, compelling, and immensely instructive. But taken as a whole, and analyzed with scientific rigor, they can be even more valuable.

To conduct that sort of analysis in a way that avoids bias, I follow a strict, complete set of patterns and code the reasons chief executive officers (CEOs) give for their company's success or failure according to these patterns. The patterns are derived from an ancient set of Chinese narratives: *The 36 Stratagems*. Together, they offer a complete toolkit for explaining and devising strategies. (You will find a full descriptive list in Appendix B.) By categorizing the stories CEOs tell into these 36 stratagems, I was able to quantify statistically how they speak and therefore how they see the world.

I began by dissecting the strategies of companies such as Dell, Southwest Airlines, and Walmart, who over the course of the 1990s radically disrupted their industries, and I found some surprising similarities in how these companies engineered breakthrough growth. The breakthrough companies of the late 1990s and early 2000s shared a unique view of their markets. I then drilled down further, conducting a rigorous top-down analysis starting with 9,000 publicly traded companies from around the world and isolating from these the 100 most competitive companies of the decade. These were 100 companies that for the

10 years ending in 2004 consistently outperformed their peers in terms of revenue growth, profit (EBITDA) margin, and shareholder returns. Again, we were struck by the similarities in their approaches. Across industries and geographies, these breakthrough companies adopted surprisingly similar playbooks when engaging their competition.

Since that 2004 study, my colleagues and I have trained more than 3,000 executives and entrepreneurs—from across the United States, Latin America, Europe, and Asia—on how to apply the findings.

Each time we apply the research, we update it, seeking out fresher competitors to learn from. Through this refreshing process, we have noticed that winning strategic patterns have started to shift. What most often led to breakthrough performance in the decade ending 2004 may not be as applicable today.

This is surely no great surprise. As this book details, the nature of competition has radically changed since 2004. Product life cycles have shortened dramatically, outsourcing has restructured entire business sectors, social media and real-time marketing have become mainstream, and competitors are crossing industry borders faster than ever before. We believe a new paradigm shift is under way. A new crop of business heroes, like Apple, Google, and Amazon, are displacing once-admired companies like Dell, GE, and Starbucks at an unprecedented rate.

Fortune Magazine's Most Admired Companies

2000	2005	2010
1. GE	1. Dell	1. Apple*
2. Microsoft	2. GE	2. Google*
3. Dell	3. Starbucks*	3. Berkshire Hathaway*
4. Cisco	4. Walmart	4. Johnson & Johnson*
5. Walmart	5. Southwest Airlines*	5. Amazon*

*Indicates a newcomer to the list.

To address the paradigm shift, I spent six months revisiting my initial analysis. To calculate which strategic patterns are working today, my colleagues and I isolated 16 companies that have delivered extraordinary performance over the past five years. These companies—including Apple, Oracle, Research in Motion, and Vistaprint—produced 40 percent revenue growth on average over the past five years, seven times that of their peers, and were three times as profitable as their competitors in term of EBITDA margin.

"Winners" and "Losers" Analyzed

Winners	Losers (Peers)
Research in Motion	Nokia
Apple	Microsoft
AT&T	Sprint
Oracle	SAP
Aflac	UNUM
Urban Outfitters	American Eagle Outfitters
Blue Nile	Tiffany's
Priceline.com	Expedia
inVentiv Health	PDI
WMS Industries	International Gaming Technologies
Concur Technologies	Ariba
Green Mountain Coffee Roasters	Caribou Coffee Company
Vistaprint	Consolidated Graphics
Hansen Natural Corporation	Dr. Pepper Snapple Group
Illumina	Beckman Coulter
Rosetta Stone	Tiffany's

By comparing these "winners" to their closest peers, using a process called narrative analysis, I was able to dissect how their strategic playbooks differ.[1] In all, I analyzed 686 strategic narratives. By isolating their most significant differences, we were able to gain insight into how today's winners see the world, choose strategies, and win.

I then deepened this core analysis by personally interviewing the CEOs of several breakthrough companies, including Aflac, Rosetta Stone, and Vistaprint, and asking them to walk us through their strategic logic.

APPENDIX B

The 36 Stratagems

For the past 10 years, I have been working with a set of strategic metaphors found in an ancient Chinese text called *The 36 Stratagems.* A full description of the stratagems, accompanied by historical and modern cases, can be found in my second book, *Hide a Dagger Behind a Smile.* Nobody knows who actually wrote the stratagems. They were developed over a period of 1,000 years, between AD 500 and 1500, through the process of oral tradition.

The stratagems represent a complete vocabulary for describing and managing competition today, and to emphasize their value as a teaching tool, I have called them strategic narratives. Following you will find a catalog of all the stratagems presented in their original language accompanied by a modern interpretation, a key strategic question that you can use to apply the stratagem, and reference to a business example that you can research if you would like more insight into how the stratagem applies to modern business competition.

	Original	Modern	Question	Example
1	**To catch something, first let it go.**	**To catch something, first let it go.**	What would happen if you let your competitor go?	Cable companies v. TiVo

(*continued*)

(continued)

	Original	Modern	Question	Example
	Press the enemy force too hard and it will strike back fiercely. Let it go and its morale will sink. Follow it closely, but do not push it too hard. Tire it and sap its morale. Then, you will be able to capture it without shedding blood. In short, a careful delay in attack will help to bring victory.	Do not attack; rather, let it go and follow close behind.		
2	**Exchange a brick for a jade.** Use bait to lure the enemy and take him in.	**Exchange a "brick" for a "jade"** Give something on which you place relatively little value in exchange for something that you value much more.	What "brick" can you give away?	HP profits from cartridges rather than printers
3	**Invite your enemy onto the roof, then remove the ladder.** Expose your weak points deliberately to entice the enemy to penetrate your line, then surround him by cutting off his exit.	**Invite him onto your roof, then remove the ladder.** Entice him to enter your domain and remove his escape route. This moves the competition into your domain.	How can you invite your adversary into your domain and remove his means of escape?	Microsoft Encarta v. Britannica
4	**Lure the tiger down from the mountain.** Use unfavorable natural conditions to	**Stay out of his stronghold.** Purposefully avoid entering his stronghold. This	What is your adversary's stronghold, and what would it	Car Max v. AutoNation

	Original	Modern	Question	Example
	trap the enemy in a difficult position. Use deception to lure him out. In an offensive that involves great risk, lure the enemy to come out against you.	will preempt resistance or, if he comes out of his stronghold to attack, will give you an advantage.	mean to stay out of it?	
5	**Befriend the distant enemy to attack one nearby.** It is more advantageous to conquer nearby enemies, because of geographical reasons, than those far away. So ally yourself temporarily with your distant enemies in spite of political differences.	**Partner with someone unexpected.** Ask yourself "Who else benefits if I win?" to see how you might partner with "competitors" or with others outside of current consideration.	Who else benefits if you win?	Hero Honda (a partnership between Honda and bicycle company)
6	**Kill with a borrowed knife.** Your enemy's situation is clear but your ally's stand is uncertain. At this time, induce your ally to attack your enemy in order to preserve your strength. In dialectic terms, another man's loss is your gain.	**Find a third party influence ("kill with a borrowed knife").** Figure out who else could influence your target and have him do so to your advantage.	What third party can influence your adversary?	Coca-Cola and the Home Sweetener Company
7	**Besiege Wei to rescue Zhao.** It is wiser to launch an attack against the	**Launch a two-front battle.** Join forces with an ally in such a way	With whom can you launch a two-front battle?	Virgin Atlantic v. British Airways

(continued)

(*continued*)

	Original	Modern	Question	Example
	enemy force when it is dispersed than to fight it when it is concentrated. He who strikes first fails, and he who strikes late prevails.	that it forces a two-front, or multi-front battle.		
8	**The stratagem of sowing discord** Use the enemy's spies to work for you and you will win without any loss inflicted on your side.	**Replace resistant relationships with a supportive one.** Find out what critical relationships resistance depends on and work on that relationship to turn it into your favor.	What critical dependency (relationship) can you remove?	Coca-Cola v. Pepsi in Venezuela
9	**Trouble the water to catch the fish.** When the enemy falls into internal chaos, exploit his weakened position and lack of direction and win him over to your side. This is as natural as people going to bed at the end of the day.	**Bundle or disaggregate.** Combine things or separate things into their parts so as to alter how they perceive you and to remove yourself from direct comparison.	What can you combine or disconnect to confuse your adversary?	Bundling or unbundling financial instruments; Microsoft Office
10	**Remove the firewood from under the pot** When confronted with a powerful enemy, do not fight him head-on, but try to find his weakest spot to	**Lock up resources.** Rather than engage in a head-on confrontation, analyze what is fueling resistance and lock up its supply.	What inputs can you control?	Apple locks up hard-drives for the first iPod.

	Original	Modern	Question	Example
	initiate his collapse. This is the weak overcoming the strong.			
11	**Shut the door to capture the thief.** When dealing with a small and weak enemy, surround and destroy him. If you let him retreat, you will be at a disadvantage in pursuing him.	**Close the exits.** When you enjoy a moment of influence, take full advantage of it and prolong it.	What moments of power can you capitalize on?	Barnes & Noble's book superstores
12	**Replace the beams with rotten timbers.** Make the allied forces change their battle formation frequently, so that their main strength will be taken away. When they collapse by themselves, go and swallow them up. This is like pulling back the wheels of a chariot to control its direction.	**Remove key support structures.** Do not take on resistance head-on but rather focus on the key supports that provide the integrity on which resistance depends.	What are the "structural beams" of resistance and how can you attack them?	Witherspoon v. large pub. companies in the UK
13	**The stratagem of the beautiful woman** When faced with a formidable enemy, try to subdue his leader. When dealing with an able	**Appeal to a key weakness or desire.** Identify a high-priority need or weakness and appeal to this to remove resistance.	What strong need or desire of your adversary's can you capitalize on?	Microsoft investments in retailers support MSN in the 1990s

(*continued*)

(*continued*)

	Original	Modern	Question	Example
	and resourceful commander, exploit his indulgence of sensual pleasures in order to weaken his fighting spirit. When the commander becomes inept, his soldiers will become demoralized, and their combat power will be greatly weakened. This stratagem takes advantage of the enemy's weakness for the sake of self-protection.			
14	**Beat the grass to startle the snake.** Any suspicion about the enemy's circumstances must be investigated. Before any military action, be sure to ascertain the enemy's situation; repeated reconnaissance is an effective way to discover the hidden enemy	**Beat the grass to startle the snake.** Launch a "false" or small-scale advance to understand what response a real advance would trigger.	What small incursion could you launch to gather information about your competition?	Microsoft's entry into servers
15	**Loot a burning house.** When the enemy falls into severe crisis, exploit his adversity and attack by direct	**Seize opportunity out of trouble.** When trouble strikes, others may freeze or retreat. Capitalize on this by advancing.	Where is there trouble, and what would happen if you advanced where others retreated?	Warren Buffett's and Carlos Slim's investment strategies

	Original	Modern	Question	Example
	confrontation. This is the strong defeating the weak.			
16	**Sometimes running away is the best strategy.** To avoid combat with a powerful enemy, the whole army should retreat and wait for the right time to advance again. This is not inconsistent with normal military principles.	**Retreat to advance later or elsewhere.** Rather than persisting with your current fight, retreat to preserve your strength and apply it somewhere else or at some other time.	From where can you retreat in order to win later?	Steve Jobs cuts Apple R&D projects to 7 from 300
17	**Seize the opportunity to lead the sheep away.** Exploit any minor lapses on the enemy side, and seize every advantage to your side. Any negligence of the enemy must be turned into a benefit for you.	**Seize the "deer in the headlights" moment.** Look for a moment when resistance is stopped by a conflicting agenda or is distracted, and move forward in the face of inaction.	What will your competition not do or defend?	iPod vs. Walkman
18	**Feign madness but keep your balance.** At times, it is better to pretend to be foolish and do nothing, than to brag about yourself and act recklessly. Be composed and plot secretly, like thunder	**Appear crazy.** In order to avoid being perceived as a threat, appear to be following an unrealistic plan or appear incapable of fulfilling it.	How can you appear "crazy"?	Richard Branson of Virgin

(*continued*)

(*continued*)

	Original	Modern	Question	Example
	clouds hiding themselves during winter only to bolt out when the time is right.			
19	**Watch the fire on the other shore.** When a serious conflict breaks out within the enemy alliance, wait quietly for the chaos to build. Because once its internal conflict intensifies, the alliance will bring destruction upon itself. As for you, observe closely and make preparations for any advantage that may come from it.	**Let them fight.** When your adversaries are engaged in conflict, refrain from acting, as this might unify resistance. Stay out of the fray, let them fight, and move in later.	What would happen if you did not push forward?	Intel avoiding entering hardware business
20	**Let the plum tree wither in place of the peach.** When loss is inevitable, sacrifice the part for the benefit of the whole.	**Sacrifice one front to win another.** Allow your adversary a victory on one front to preserve, even strengthen, your competitiveness on another front.	What can you sacrifice?	Qualcomm exits hardware and infra-structure
21	**The stratagem of the open city gates** In spite of the inferiority of your force, deliberately make your defensive	**Reveal your strategy.** Openly reveal your strength, weakness, or strategy to encourage your	What would happen if you revealed your strategy in the open?	Vaporware; iPad v. HP and Microsoft tablets

	Original	Modern	Question	Example
	line defenseless in order to confuse the enemy. In situations when the enemies are many and you are few, this tactic seems all the more intriguing.	adversary to call off his attack (e.g., because he fears your strength or no longer considers you a threat).		
22	**Await the exhausted enemy at your ease.** To weaken the enemy, it is not necessary to attack him directly. Tire him by carrying out an active defense and in so doing his strength will be reduced and your side will gain the upper hand.	**Move early to the next battleground.** Identify the next battleground, set up a defendable position there, and wait for the others. When they arrive, use your superior position to win.	Where is the next battleground?	Rosetta Stone in language software
23	**Exchange the role of guest for that of host.** Whenever there is a chance, enter into the decision-making body of your ally and extend your influence skillfully step-by-step. Eventually, put it under your control.	**Exchange the role of guest for that of host.** Take an unthreatening stance then incrementally build trust and influence.	How can you move up the decision-making chain of your customers/ adversary?	SharePoint's free version
24	**Borrow the road to conquer Gao.** When a small state, located between two big states, is being	**Borrow a road.** Look for someone who has better access to your objective. Create an	Whose road could you borrow? Who is borrowing your road?	Legend (now Lenovo) v. HP; Google v. Motorola

(*continued*)

(*continued*)

	Original	Modern	Question	Example
	threatened by the enemy state, you should immediately send troops to rescue it, thereby expanding your sphere of influence. Mere talk cannot win the trust of a state in a difficult position.	alliance with them to gain passage.		
25	**Shed your skin like the golden cicada.** Make your front array appear as if you are still holding your position so that the allied force will not suspect your intention and the enemy troops will not dare to attack rashly. Then withdraw your main forces secretly.	**Create a façade then move the action.** Create a façade that appears to be the real thing, then move the action somewhere else.	If your current activity were an empty shell, to where could you move the action?	Best Buy profits from service not selling electronics
26	**The stratagem of injuring yourself** People rarely inflict injuries on themselves, so when they get injured, it is usually genuine. Exploit this naivete to make the enemy believe your words; then sowing discord within enemy ranks will work. In this case, one takes advantage of the	**Injure yourself.** Injure yourself to either (1) win trust or (2) avoid appearing a threat.	How would the competition respond if you injured yourself?	Intel v. IBM in the first PC

	Original	Modern	Question	Example
	enemy's weakness, and makes the enemy look as if he were a naive child who is easily taken.			
27	**Borrow a corpse for the soul's return.** The powerful is beyond exploitation, but the weak needs help. Exploit and manipulate the weak for they need you more than you need them.	**Embrace what others abandoned.** Adopt a forgotten or abandoned model, idea, or technology to differentiate yourself and build power.	What has been abandoned?	BlackBerry uses abandoned pager network
28	**Point at the mulberry but curse the locust.** When the powerful wants to rule over the weak, he will sound a warning. One's uncompromising stand will often win loyalty, and one's resolute action, respect.	**Send a covert message.** Rather than attack directly, aim your effort at a different target. This will send a covert message to your real target that will alter his behavior.	What "covert message" could you send?	Price guarantees
29	**Clamor in the east; attack to the west.** When the enemy command is in confusion, it will be unprepared for contingencies. The situation is like flood waters rising higher and higher; likely to burst the dam at any	**Clamor in the east; attack to the west.** Feign an approach the defense of which exposes your target to a different (true) attack. Fake left, move right.	What fake attack could you launch; would this expose your adversary to an alternative attack?	The Flick Group takeover of Feldmühle Nobel

(*continued*)

(continued)

	Original	Modern	Question	Example
	moment. When the enemy loses internal control, take the chance to destroy him.			
30	**Openly repair the walkway, secretly march to Chen Cang.** To pin down the enemy, expose part of your action deliberately, so that you can make a surprise attack somewhere else.	**Take the unorthodox path.** When others are focused on the direct, orthodox approach, use an indirect, unorthodox path to take them by surprise.	What is the obvious path; what if you took the unorthodox path?	Dell goes direct
31	**Fool the emperor and cross the sea.** The perception of perfect preparation leads to relaxed vigilance. Familiar sights lead to slackened suspicion. Therefore, secret machinations are better concealed in the open than in the dark, and extreme public exposure often contains extreme secrecy.	**Hide in the open.** Make your actions appear normal (i.e., appear to be everyday actions) so that others will not see that something new is coming.	What are the everyday activities in which you could hide your actions?	Disney purchases land for Disneyworld
32	**Create something out of nothing.** Design a counterfeit front to put the enemy off guard. When the trick works, the front is	**Create something out of nothing.** When the direct approach (i.e., one using existing players) is ineffective, create a	What player do you wish was in the game?	White Day in Japan and South Korea

	Original	Modern	Question	Example
	changed into something real so that the enemy will be thrown into a state of double confusion. In short, deceptive appearances often conceal forthcoming danger.	new player or entity "out of nothing" to change the dynamic in your favor.		
33	**Hide a dagger behind a smile.** One way or another, make the enemies trust you and thereby slacken their vigilance. Meanwhile, plot secretly, making preparations for your future action to ensure its success.	**Be good.** Because a threat will generate resistance, choose an approach that is, or appears to be, friendly. You thereby transform resistance into pull.	How could you appear or truly be helpful?	Google v. Yahoo! and Alta Vista
34	**Deck the tree with bogus blossoms.** Use deceptive appearances to make your troop formation look more powerful than it is. When wild geese soar high above, the grandness of their formation is greatly enhanced by the display of their outstretched wings.	**Coordinate the uncoordinated.** Combine and coordinate independent elements within your environment to orchestrate much greater power.	Who could you coordinate?	Wikipedia
35	**To catch the bandits, capture their leader.** Capture their chief, and the enemy will	**Focus influence on the leader.** Rather than influence the entire organization,	What unique needs does your adversary's leader hold?	Rupert Murdoch v. John Malone in battle for DirectTV

(*continued*)

(*continued*)

	Original	Modern	Question	Example
	collapse. His situation will be as desperate as a sea dragon fighting on land.	identify and incent just the leader(s). This is like leading a horse by directing its head.		
36	**The stratagem of linking stratagems** When the enemy possesses a superior force, do not attack recklessly. Instead, weaken him by devising plots to bring him into a difficult position of his own doing. Good leadership plays a key role in winning a war. A wise commander gains Heaven's favor.	**Link strategies.** Rather than execute one strategy, execute multiple strategies (simultaneously or in succession). If one strategy is not effective, the next one is. If the next one is not effective, the following one is.	What strategies could you combine?	Apple's iPod strategies

APPENDIX C

Tools

Here are a set of worksheets you can use to apply the Outthinker Process laid out in Part 4 of this book. You can get updated copies of these worksheets from www.kaihan.net.

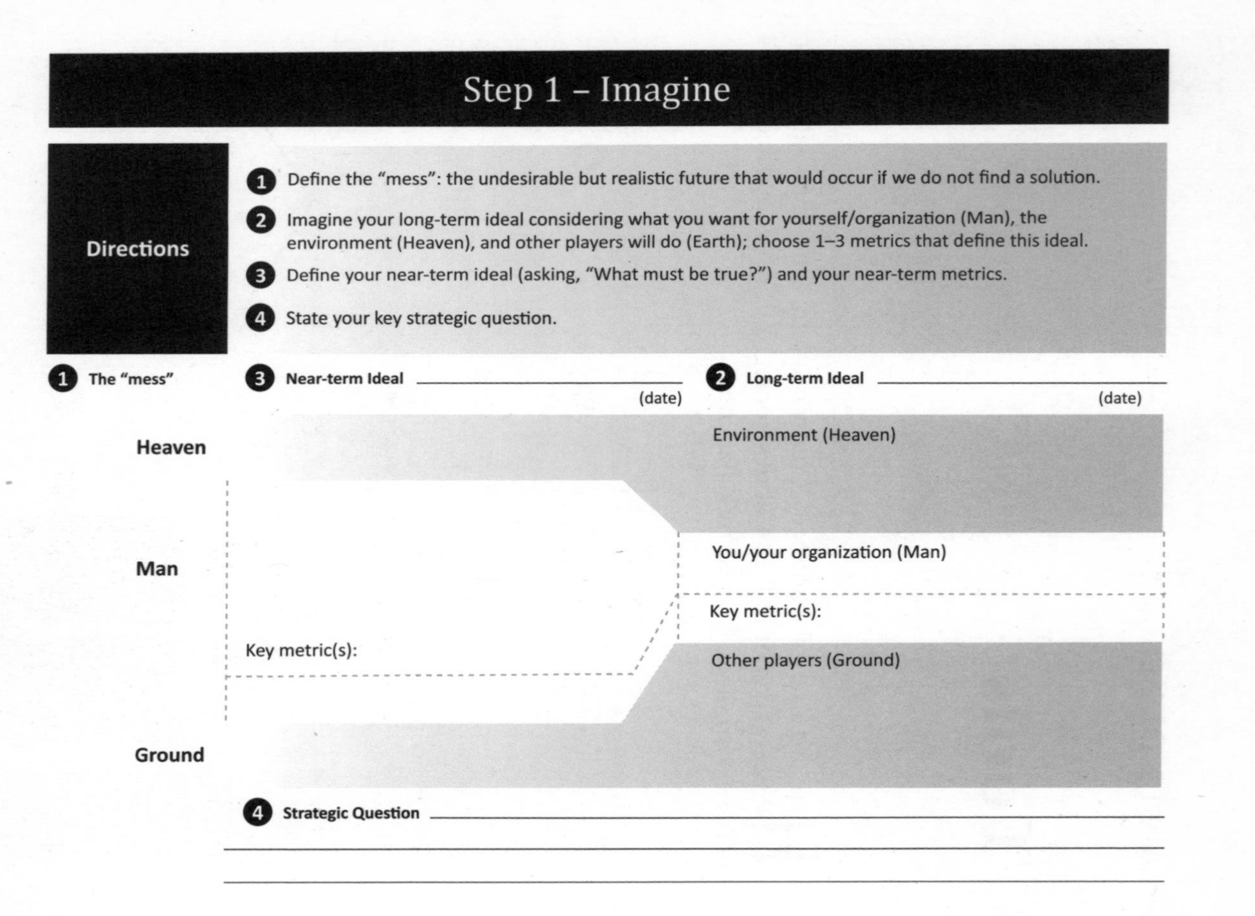
Step 1 – Imagine
Directions
1 Define the "mess": the undesirable but realistic future that would occur if we do not find a solution.
2 Imagine your long-term ideal considering what you want for yourself/organization (Man), the environment (Heaven), and other players will do (Earth); choose 1–3 metrics that define this ideal.
3 Define your near-term ideal (asking, "What must be true?") and your near-term metrics.
4 State your key strategic question.
1 The "mess"
3 Near-term Ideal
(date)
2 Long-term Ideal
(date)
Heaven
Environment (Heaven)
Man
You/your organization (Man)
Key metric(s):
Key metric(s):
Other players (Ground)
Ground
4 Strategic Question

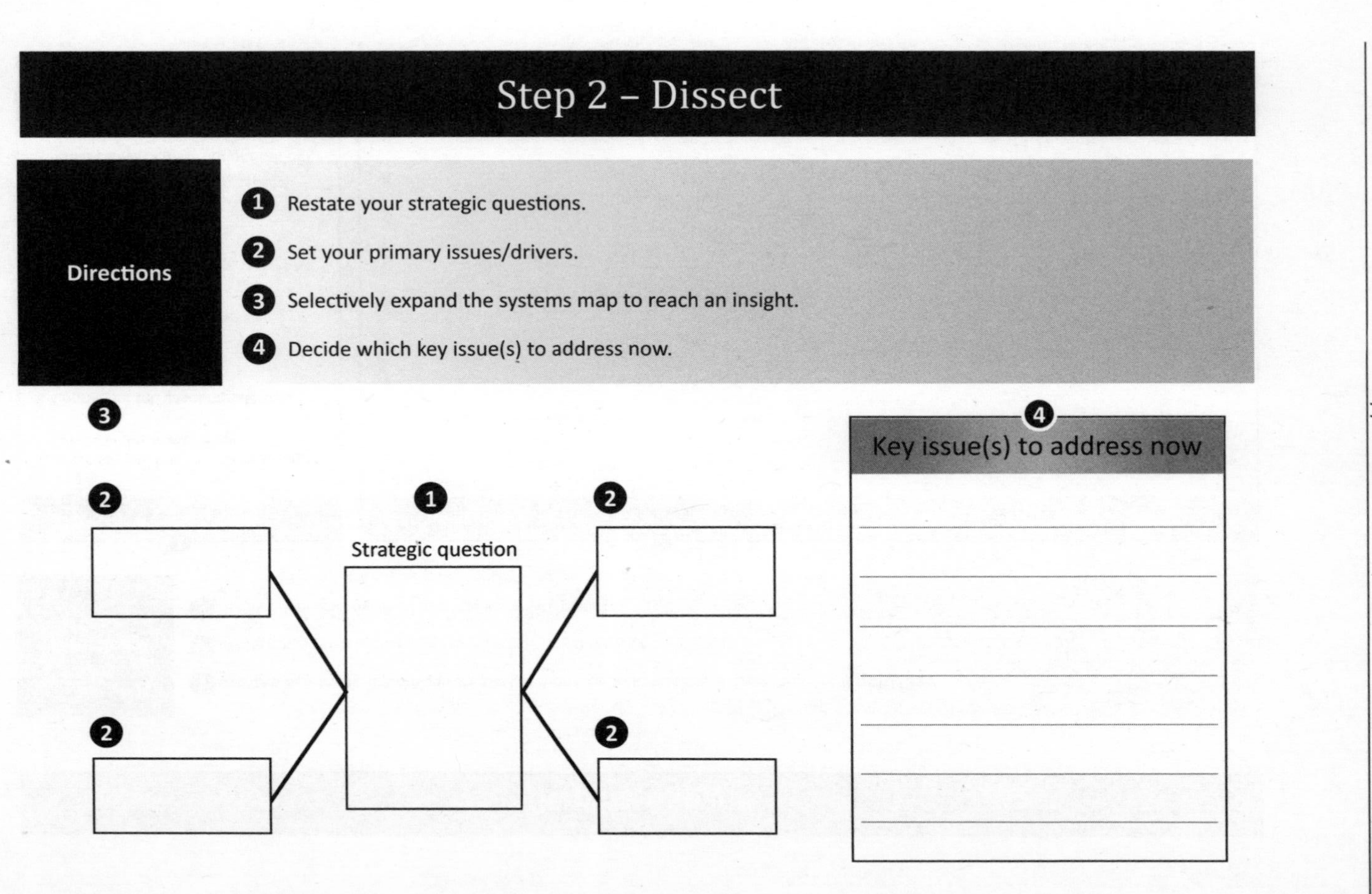
Step 2 – Dissect
Directions
1 Restate your strategic questions.
2 Set your primary issues/drivers.
3 Selectively expand the systems map to reach an insight.
4 Decide which key issue(s) to address now.
3
2
1 Strategic question
2
2
2
4 Key issue(s) to address now

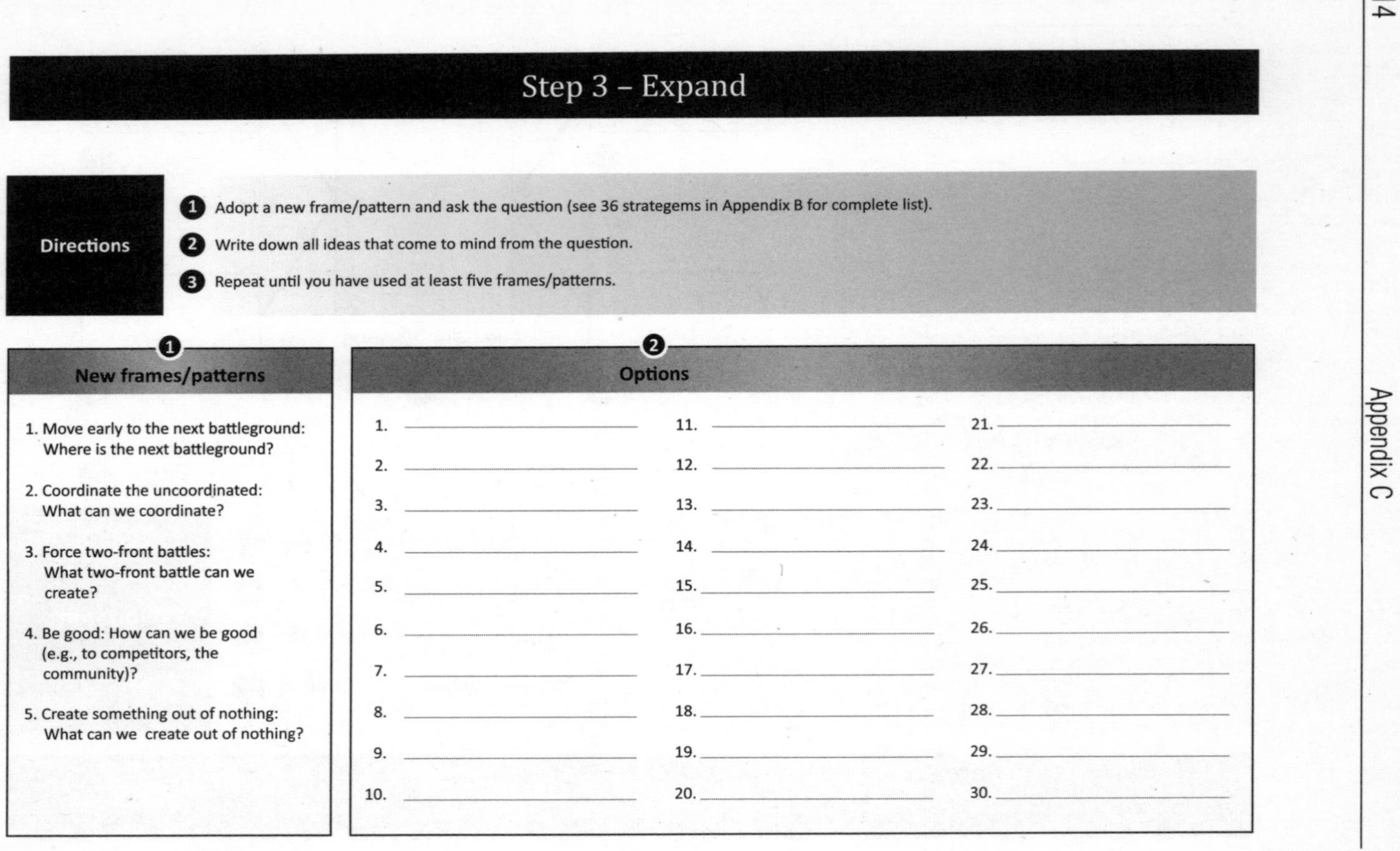

Step 3 – Expand

Directions

1. Adopt a new frame/pattern and ask the question (see 36 strategems in Appendix B for complete list).
2. Write down all ideas that come to mind from the question.
3. Repeat until you have used at least five frames/patterns.

❶ New frames/patterns	❷ Options		
1. Move early to the next battleground: Where is the next battleground?	1. ______	11. ______	21. ______
	2. ______	12. ______	22. ______
2. Coordinate the uncoordinated: What can we coordinate?	3. ______	13. ______	23. ______
	4. ______	14. ______	24. ______
3. Force two-front battles: What two-front battle can we create?	5. ______	15. ______	25. ______
	6. ______	16. ______	26. ______
4. Be good: How can we be good (e.g., to competitors, the community)?	7. ______	17. ______	27. ______
	8. ______	18. ______	28. ______
5. Create something out of nothing: What can we create out of nothing?	9. ______	19. ______	29. ______
	10. ______	20. ______	30. ______

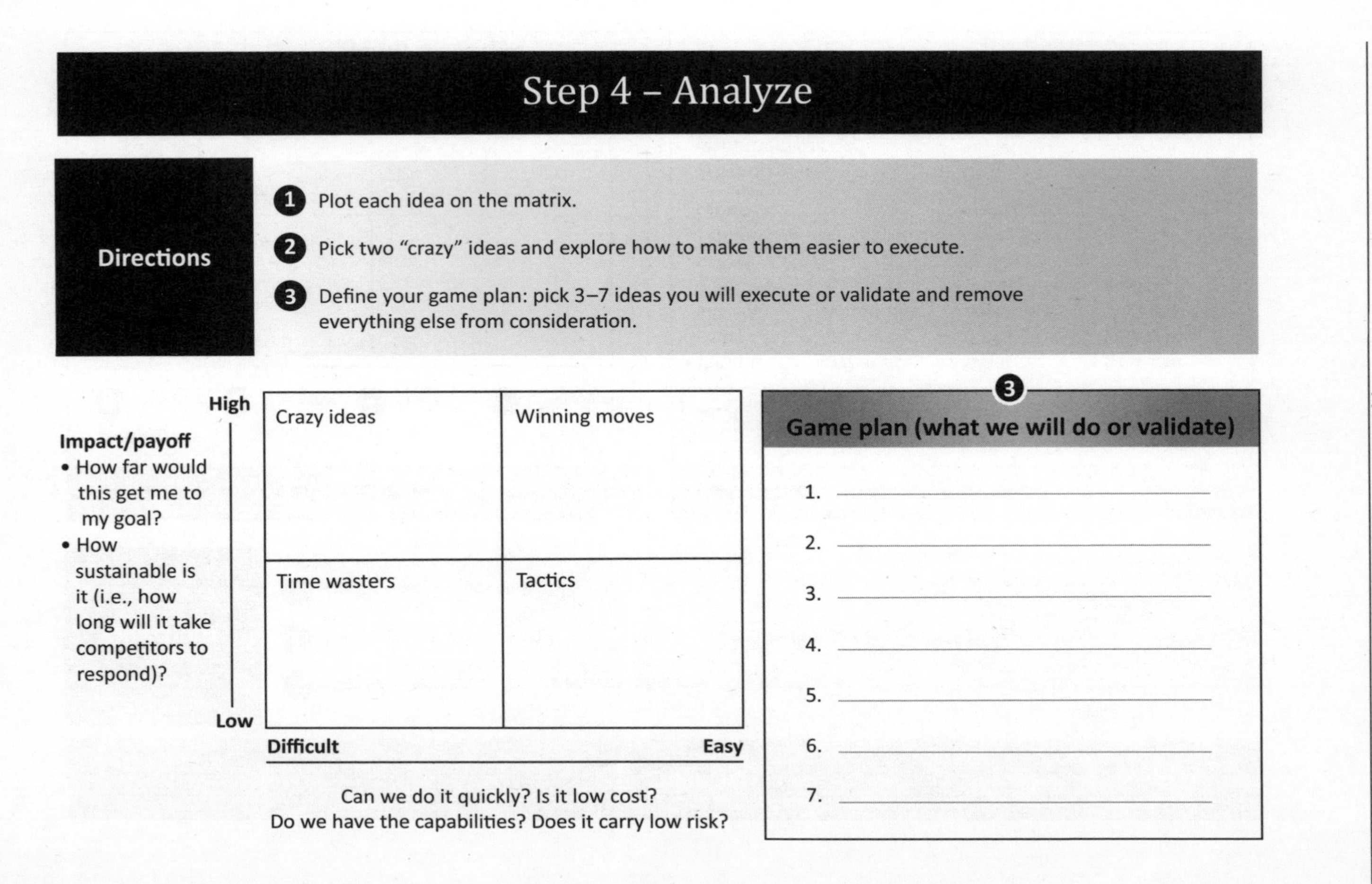

Step 4 – Analyze
Directions
1 Plot each idea on the matrix.
2 Pick two "crazy" ideas and explore how to make them easier to execute.
3 Define your game plan: pick 3–7 ideas you will execute or validate and remove everything else from consideration.
Impact/payoff
• How far would this get me to my goal?
• How sustainable is it (i.e., how long will it take competitors to respond)?
High
Low
Crazy ideas
Winning moves
Time wasters
Tactics
Difficult
Easy
Can we do it quickly? Is it low cost?
Do we have the capabilities? Does it carry low risk?
3 Game plan (what we will do or validate)
1.
2.
3.
4.
5.
6.
7.

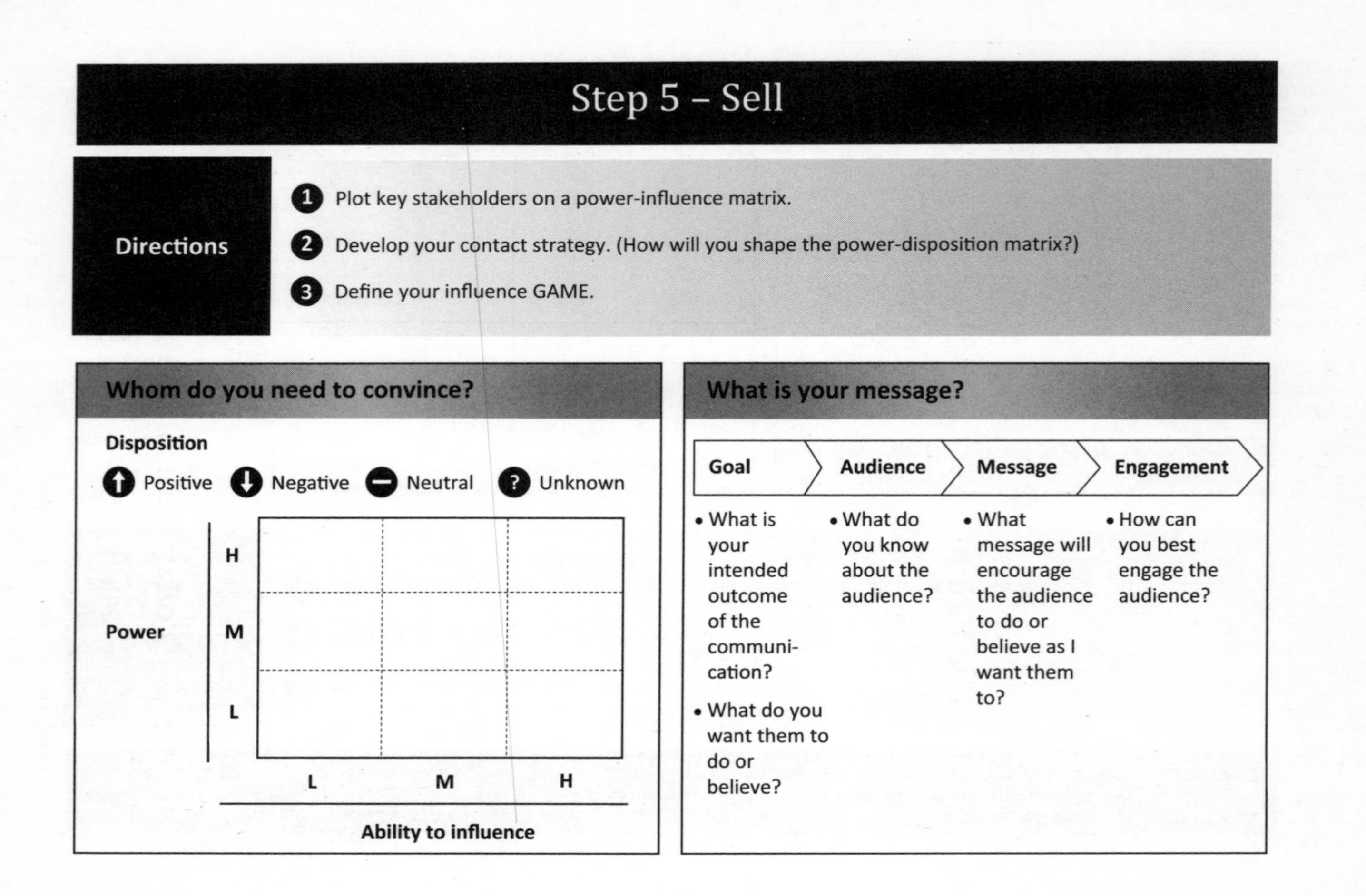
Step 5 – Sell
Directions
1 Plot key stakeholders on a power-influence matrix.
2 Develop your contact strategy. (How will you shape the power-disposition matrix?)
3 Define your influence GAME.
Whom do you need to convince?
Disposition
Positive
Negative
Neutral
Unknown
Power
H
M
L
L
M
H
Ability to influence
What is your message?
Goal
Audience
Message
Engagement
• What is your intended outcome of the communi-cation?
• What do you want them to do or believe?
• What do you know about the audience?
• What message will encourage the audience to do or believe as I want them to?
• How can you best engage the audience?

NOTES

Part 1 The Foundation

1. Max Planck, *Age, Ageing and Age Structure in Science* (Chicago: The University of Chicago Press, 1973), 514.

Chapter 1 Evolution through Revolution

1. John Boyd, *A Discourse of Winning and Losing*, U.S. Air Force presentation, July/August 1992.
2. John Markoff, "Technology: Loving Google But Not Its Public Offering," the *New York Times,* Aug. 6, 2004.
3. Ibid.
4. Ibid.
5. Bevin Alexander, *How Great Generals Win* (New York: Norton, 1993).
6. Oregon State University Alumni Association website, http://oregonstate.edu/portlandmetro/portlandalumni.html (accessed May 24, 2001); Olympic Committee website, http://www.olympic.org/html (accessed May 24, 2001).
7. Harry Cross, "Notre Dame's Open Play Amazes Army," *New York Times,* November 2, 1913.
8. Ibid.
9. Muhammad Yunus in interview with *Nightly Business Report,* reported in Knowledge@Wharton, "Muhammad Yunus, Banker to the World's Poorest Citizens, Makes His Case," March 9, 2005, http://knowledge.wharton.upenn.edu/article.cfm?articleid=1147 (accessed August 23, 2011).

Chapter 2 Today's Business Revolution

1. Niccoló Machiavelli, *The Prince.* (New York: Oxford University Press,1979), 75.
2. Shoshana Zuboff, "Creating Value Distributed Capitalism Resonates with Value Network Logic and Principles," *McKinsey Quarterly*, September 27, 2010.

3. Cisco Systems estimate, as reported by McKinsey & Company.
4. Reported on MSNBC, March 23, 2011.
5. Tim Arango, "Time Warner Takes a Shot at Netflix," *New York Times,* December 13, 2010.
6. McKinsey Global Survey, "Forces Shaping the World," *The McKinsey Quarterly,* May 18, 2010.
7. McKinsey Global Survey, "Five Forces Reshaping the Global Economy: McKinsey Global Survey Results," *The McKinsey Quarterly,* May 2010.

Part 2 The New Outthinker Playbook

1. Marcus Aurelius, *The Meditations*, Book 9, trans. George Long (Guildford, United Kingdom: White Crow Books, 2010).
2. Wang Chen, *The Tao of War: The Martial Tao Te Ching,* trans. Ralph D. Sawyer (Boulder, CO: Westview Press, 2003).

Chapter 3 Move Early to the Next Battleground

1. Sun Tzu, *The Art of War: The Denma Translation* (Boston: Shambala, 2001), 191.
2. Author interview of Tom Adams on September 14, 2010.
3. Steve Jobs, "Magic Kingdom: How Apple's Demanding Visionary Will Shake up Disney and the World of Entertainment," *BusinessWeek*, February 6, 2006.

Chapter 4 Coordinate the Uncoordinated

1. Thomas Huynh, *The Art of War: Spirituality for Conflict* (Woodstock, VT: SkyLight Paths Publishing, 2009).
2. Niccoló Machiavelli, *The Prince* as published in *Classics of Moral and Political Theory*. (Indianapolis, IN: Hackett Publishing Company, Inc., 1992), 553.
3. Author interview of Blane Walter on February 10, 2010.
4. Author interview of Glenn Richardson on December 22, 2010.
5. Attivio company website, www.attivio.com, (accessed September 2010).

Chapter 5 Force Two-Front Battles

1. Sun Tzu, trans. Thomas Huynh, *Art of War,* Chapter 6, (Woodstock, VT: SkyLight Paths Publishing, 2009).
2. Author interview of *Wall Street Journal* executive, name held in confidence, on May 14, 2010.

3. Mark Vadon, "How I Got People to Buy Diamonds on the Web," Fast Company, http://www.fastcompany.com/events/realtime/miami/blog/vadon.html.
4. Value Line report on Blue Nile, February 19, 2010.
5. Diana Irvine (CEO of Blue Nile), in discussion with the author, April 1, 2010.
6. Author interview of Diane Irvine on April 1, 2010.
7. Author interview of Ajit Prabhu on August 11, 2009.
8. Ibid.
9. Ibid.

Chapter 6 Be Good

1. Michael Milken, www.mikemilken.com (accessed on Aug 19, 2011).
2. Confucius, *Analects II*, 1, online version, http://www.analects.org/analects/analectschaptertwo.html, (accessed August 28, 2011).
3. Stephanie Clifford, "Where Wal-Mart Failed, Aldi Succeeds," *New York Times*, March 29, 2011.
4. Author interview of Dr. Marco Iacoboni, March 18, 2009.
5. William Shakespeare, The *Works of William Shakspeare; Containing His Plays and Poems, To Which is Added a Glossary*. (London, 1797), 562.
6. Napoleon Bonaparte, *The Book of Positive Quotations*. (Edmonton, Canada: Rubicon Press Inc, 1993), 373.
7. Michael Feiner, *The Feiner Points of Leadership*, presentation at the "Outthinker Network" in New York, May 6, 2011.
8. Michael Milken, "Official Biography of Michael Milken" http://www.mikemilken.com/biography.taf. (accessed August 31, 2011).
9. Michael Milken, "Creating Value," http://www.mikemilken.com/articles.taf?page=32.

Chapter 7 Create Something Out of Nothing

1. Louise Nevelson, *The Book of Positive Quotations*. (Edmonton, Canada: Rubicon Press Inc, 1993).
2. Steven Pinker, *The Blank Slate: The Modern Denial of Human Nature* (London: Penguin Books, 2002), 202.
3. Justin Schreck and Ben Worthen, "Dell Inc. Lowers Its Sights for Gadgets, Consumers," *Wall Street Journal*, May 23, 2011.
4. Eric Eldon, "Zynga's Pre-paid Virtual Currency Cards Have Expanded to More Than 12,800 US Stores," Insidesocialgames.com, March 25, 2010.
5. Paul Glimcher, *Wisdom: From Philosophy to Neuroscience*. (New York: Random House, 2010), 88.
6. Author interview of Daniel Amos, CEO of Aflac, on March 2, 2010, New York, NY.

Chapter 8 Mental Time Travel

1. V. S. Naipaul, http://thinkexist.com/quotation/most_people_are_not_really_free-they_are_confined/151743.html, (accessed August 28, 2011).
2. Louis Antoine Fauvelet de Bourrienne, *Memoirs of Napoleon Bonaparte* (London: Richard Bentley, 1836), 4:244.
3. Author interview with Alexandra Kosteniuk on April 10, 2010, via e-mail.
4. Thomas Huynh, *Art of War: Spirituality for Conflict* (Woodstock, VT: Skylight Paths, Chapter 10, 2008).
5. Henry Kissinger, *On China* (New York: Penguin, 2011), 530.
6. Robert A. Caro, *Master of the Senate,* vol. 3, *The Years of Lyndon Johnson* (New York: Vintage Books, Random House, 2002), 531.
7. Bob Benson, "Other People's Words," LuLu.com Press, 2008, 55.
8. Alan Ohnsman, "Detroit Auto No-Shows Put Startups Fisker, Tesla in Spotlight," *Bloomberg.com,* January 19, 2009.
9. Tesla Motors website, http://www.teslamotors.com/blog/secret-tesla-motors-master-plan-just-between-you-and-me, August 3, 2006.
10. "Tesla Worth a Half Billion Dollars after Daimler Investment," techcrunch.com, May 19, 2009.
11. "Tesla IPO Raises 226.1 Million," *Wired.com,* June 2010.

Chapter 9 Attacking the Interconnected System

1. Russell L. Ackoff and Frederick E. Emery, *On Purposeful Systems* (Chicago: Aldine-Atherton, 1972).
2. Julius Caesar, *Commentaries on the Gallic War.* Translated by W.A. McDevitte an W.S. Bohn (New York: Harper & Brothers, 1869).
3. David W. Barber, *The Music Lover's Quotation Book,* (Toronto, Canada: Sound And Vision Publishers, 2003), 31.
4. John Markoff, "Loving Google but Not Its Public Offering," the *New York Times,* August 6, 2004.

Chapter 10 Frame Shifting

1. Albert Einstein, As reported on quotationspage.com, http://www.quotationspage.com/quote/30373.html, (accessed August 23, 2011).
2. Paul J. Feltovich, Michael J. Prietula, and K. Anders Ericsson, *Studies of Expertise from Psychological Perspectives, The Cambridge Handbook of Expertise and Expert Performance* (Cambridge: Cambridge University Press, 2006), 57–58.

3. S. Shipp, "The Brain Circuitry of Attention," *Trends in Cognitive Sciences* 8 (2004): 223–230.
4. V. Lamme, "Why Visual Attention and Awareness Are Different," *Trends in Cognitive Sciences* 7, no. 1 (2003): 12–18.
5. Frendand Gobet and Neil Charnes, *Expertise in Chess, The Cambridge Handbook of Expertise and Expert Performance* (Cambridge: Cambridge University Press, 2006), 526.
6. A. Brown, "A Review of the Tip-of-the-Tongue Experience," *Psychological Bulletin* 109 (1991): 204–223.
7. Feltovich, *Studies of Expertise,* 50.
8. Kaihan Krippendorff, *The Way of Innovation* (Avon, MA: Adams Median, 2008).

Chapter 11 A Disruptive Mind-Set

1. Chanakya (Indian guru considered the Machiavelli of India), *The Arthashastra,* Book X "Relating to War," Chapter 5, trans. R. Shamasastry (Bangalore: Government Press, 1915).
2. Walter R. Newell, *The Soul of a Leader* (New York: Harper, 2009), 318.
3. Bruce Greenwald, *Competition Demystified* (New York: Penguin, 2007), 28.
4. Author interview with Josh Linkner, CEO of ePrize, on October 20, 2009.

Chapter 12 Shaping Perceptions

1. Albert Einstein, http://thinkexist.com/quotation/reality_is_merely_an_illusion-although_a_very/184098.html, (accessed August 23, 2011).
2. Balthasar Gracian, *The Art of Worldly Wisdom,* (New York: Bantam Doubleday Publishing, 1992), translator Christopher Maurer, Chapter 26.
3. Mohammad Yunus in interview with *Nightly Business Report*, reported in Knowledge@Wharton, "Muhammad Yunus, Banker to the World's Poorest Citizens, Makes His Case", March 9, 2005, http://knowledge.wharton.upenn.edu/article.cfm?articleid=1147, accessed August 23, 2011.
4. As quoted in Maartens, Willie, *Mapping Reality: A Critical Perspective on Science and Religion*, (Lincoln, NE: iUniverse, 2006), 364.
5. Author interview of Dr. Marco Iacoboni, March 18, 2009.
6. Ibid.

Chapter 13 Step 1: Imagine

1. George Bernard Shaw, (n.d.), http://www.1-famousquotes.com/quote/11879, (accessed August 23, 2011).

2. Napoleon Bonaparte, (n.d.), http://www.1-famous-quotes.com/quote/3497351, (accessed August 23, 2011).
3. Clayton, Brown, "Clayton Brown's Founders' Day essay," April 12, 2006, http://news.stanford.edu/news/2006/april12/brown-041206.html, (accessed August 23, 2011).
4. Tom Ford (director of *A Single Man* and former creative director at Gucci), interviewed on *Talk Asia*, CNN, June 1, 2011. Available online at http://edition.cnn.com/2011/BUSINESS/06/01/tom.ford.interview/index.html.

Chapter 14 Step 2: Dissect

1. Lao Tzu, *The Tao Te Ching,* Verse 28. Translation by R.L. Wing in The Tao of Power. (New York: Broadway Books, 1986), 71.

Chapter 15 Step 3: Expand

1. Thich Hanh, (n.d.), http://www.1-famous-quotes.com/quote/120747912. (accessed August 23, 2011).
2. Mao Tse-tung, (n.d.), http://www.1-famous-quotes.com/quote/138669. (accessed August 23, 2011).

Chapter 16 Step 4: Analyze

1. Douglas MacArthur, As quoted in James Charlton *The Military Quotation Book, Revised and Expanded: More than 1,200 of the Best Quotations About War, Leadership, Courage, Victory, and Defeat* (New York: St. Martin's Press, 2002), 10.

Chapter 17 Step 5: Sell

1. David Ogilvy and Sir Alan Parker, *Confessions of an Advertising Man* (London: Southbank Publishing, 2004), 48.
2. Muhammad Yunus in interview with *Nightly Business Report*, reported in Knowledge@Wharton, "Muhammad Yunus, Banker to the World's Poorest Citizens, Makes His Case," March 9, 2005, http://knowledge.wharton.upenn.edu/article.cfm?articleid=1147, (accessed August 23, 2011).

Chapter 18 Phase 1: Establish Multiple Points of Differentiation

1. Alexander the Great, as quoted by Hagopian Institute, *Quote Junkie: Enormous Quote Book: Over 3000 Quotes from Several Hundred of the Most Famous People in the History of the World* (Seattle, WA: CreateSpace, 2009), 11.

Chapter 19 Phase 2: Create Playbook Asymmetry

1. Leo Gough, *Miyamoto Musashi's The Book of Five Rings: A Modern-Day Interpretation of a Strategy Classic* (Oxford: Infinite Ideas, p. 2009), 30.
2. Antoine-Henri Jomini, *Art of War*. Translated by G. H. Mendell and W. P. Craighill (Rockville, MD: Arc Manor, 2007), 12.

Chapter 20 Phase 3: Construct an Outthinker Culture

1. Balthasar Gracian, *The Art of Worldly Wisdom*. (New York: Bantam Doubleday Publishing, 1992), translator Christopher Maurer, Chapter 17.
2. Napoleon Bonaparte, Napoleon Bonaparte. (n.d.), http://www.1-famous-quotes.com/quote/18623, (accessed August 24, 2011).
3. Herry Yogaswara and Eko Yulianto, "Local Knowledge of Tsunami among the Simeulue Community, Nangroe Aceh Darusallam" (Tsunami Information Center, April 2010).
4. See, for example, Michael Vlahos, *Fighting Identity* (Westport, CT: Praeger, 2009).
5. Martin L. Martins, Jennifer Jennings, and P. Devereaux Jennings, "Do the Stories They Tell Get Them the Money They Need?" *Academy of Management Journal* 50, no. 5 (2007): 1107–1132.
6. Stephen Denning, "Telling Tales," *Harvard Business Review,* May 2005.
7. See, for example, David M. Boje, "Notes on the Strategic Stories Fad," June 29, 1999, http://cbae.nmsu.edu/~dboje/strategic.html.
8. Ann Swinder, "Culture in Action: Symbols and Strategies," *American Sociology Review* 51(1986), 273–286.
9. Ulf Hannerz, *Soulside: Inquiries in Ghetto Culture and Community* (New York: Columbia University Press, 1969).
10. Danny Miller, "The Architecture of Simplicity," *Academy of Management Review* 18 (1993): 116–138.
11. Howard Gardener, *Leading Minds: An Anatomy of Leadership* (New York: Basic Books, 1995); and Joseph Campbell, *The Hero's Journey* (New York: HarperCollins, 1990).
12. See, for example, Michael G. Jacobides, "Strategy Tools for a Shifting Landscape," *Harvard Business Review* (January–February 2010): 76–84.
13. Gordon Shaw, Robert Brown, and Philip Bromiley, "Strategic Stories: How 3M Is Rewriting Business Planning," *Harvard Business Review*. 76, no. 3 (May–June 1998).
14. Patience Wheatcroft, "Sage Advice on Making an Acquisition," *Wall Street Journal,* March 2, 2010.

15. D. W. Winnicott, *Playing and Reality* (London: Tavistock Publications, 1974).
16. Richard Lyons (former chief learning officer at Goldman Sachs and now dean of the Haas School of Business at Berkeley), in discussion with the author, April 14, 2010.
17. Author interview with Kathleen Cattrall, Vice President of Branded Customer Service at Time Warner Cable, March 5, 2010.
18. Data provided by Time Warner Cable in April 2010.

Appendix A The Research

1. For more on narrative analysis, see Catherine K. Riesman, *Narrative Analysis* (Thousand Oaks, CA: Sage, 1993); and Y. Gabriel, "Narratives, Stories and Texts," in *The Sage Handbook of Organizational Discourse,* eds. Cynthia Hardy, Cliff Oswick, and Linda Putnam (London: Sage, 2004), 61–77.

INDEX